Columbia College Library
Columbia, Missouri

OF WORLDS BEYOND

The Science of
Science Fiction Writing

OF WORLDS BEYOND

The Science of Science Fiction Writing

A Symposium By

Robert A. Heinlein
John Taine
Jack Williamson
A. E. van Vogt
L. Sprague de Camp
Edward E. Smith, Ph.D.
John W. Campbell, Jr.

Edited By
Lloyd Arthur Eshbach

Chicago: 1964

Library of Congress Catalog Card No. 64-57013

Standard Book Number 911682-05-8

Copyright ©, 1947, by Fantasy Press

Copyright ©, 1964, by Lloyd Arthur Eshbach

All rights in this book are reserved. It may not be used for any purpose without written authorization from the holder of these rights. Nor may the book or any part thereof be reproduced in any manner whatsoever without permission in writing, except for brief quotations used in critical articles and reviews. For information, address: ADVENT:PUBLISHERS, INC., Post Office Box 9228, Chicago, Illinois 60690. Manufactured in the U.S.A. by Malloy Lithographing, Inc., Ann Arbor, Michigan 48106.

SECOND EDITION, September 1964
SECOND PRINTING, April 1970

CONTENTS

INTRODUCTION	9
ON THE WRITING OF SPECULATIVE FICTION . . *By Robert A. Heinlein*	11
WRITING A SCIENCE NOVEL . . . . . *By John Taine*	21
THE LOGIC OF FANTASY . . . . . . *By Jack Williamson*	37
COMPLICATION IN THE SCIENCE FICTION STORY . *By A. E. van Vogt*	51
HUMOR IN SCIENCE FICTION . . . . . *By L. Sprague de Camp*	67
THE EPIC OF SPACE . . . . *By Edward E. Smith, Ph.D.*	77
THE SCIENCE OF SCIENCE FICTION WRITING . . *By John W. Campbell, Jr.*	89

INTRODUCTION

STORIES OF WORLDS BEYOND the limits of here and now are as old as human imagination. The folklore and myths of primitive peoples, the Utopian romances of the nineteenth century, the speculative novels of Verne and Wells—all are tales of worlds beyond actuality.

During the past twenty years, speculative fiction has acquired a new form and pattern, in harmony with an age in which science and its developments have had so tremendous an influence on the lives of men. In two decades this class of writing has acquired a name—science fiction—and has gained for itself a permanent place in contemporary prose.

Since the appearance of the first science fiction magazine in 1926, the field as a whole has experienced a slow, healthy growth. In the early days a wild idea and a smattering of science sufficed to produce a salable science fiction story. But the speculative tale has outgrown its swaddling clothes, and is rapidly approaching or has already reached maturity. It appears to be well on its way toward becoming *the* fiction of the Atomic Age.

Writers and would-be writers of science fiction have long recognized the need for a practical guide, a handbook, on the writing of this new form of literature. To fill this need, seven of the recognized leaders in the field were asked to contribute their opinions on one or another phase of the subject. And since each wrote about the type of story for which he is famous, stories which differ materially from those of the other contributors to the volume, this symposium presents a varied, yet consistent, discussion of science fiction writing. It may truly be called an authoritative work on the writing of stories "Of Worlds Beyond".

LLOYD ARTHUR ESHBACH

ON THE WRITING OF SPECULATIVE FICTION

By Robert A. Heinlein

Editor's Preface

ROBERT A. HEINLEIN

ROBERT A. HEINLEIN —who is also Anson MacDonald, Caleb Saunders, John Riverside, Lyle Monroe and Simon York—was originally a Missourian. Born in Butler, Missouri, (he won't say when), he received his early schooling in the public schools of Kansas City. He learned to play chess before he learned to read, and it is his intention to take up chess again when his eyes play out.

Originally, the stars were his goal; he planned to be an astronomer. But something slipped and he landed in the U. S. Naval Academy instead. He spent not quite ten years in the Navy, was disabled, and retired. Thereafter he tried a number of things—silver mining, real estate, politics, and some graduate study in physics and math. Finally, more or less by accident, he wrote a science fiction story, calling it "Life-Line". It sold and was published in *Astounding Science Fiction* in 1939. He sold his next effort, and, in his own words, he "was hooked, having discovered a pleasant way to live without working."

From 1939 to 1942 Heinlein produced numerous stories under his several names. As Robert A. Heinlein he wrote a series of stories—short stories, novelettes and novels—all of them rather closely related, fitting into the general scheme of a carefully charted "future history". This background, which covered a two thousand year period of the future, gave Heinlein a technical and sociological basis for a consistent, unified picture of the days which lie ahead, and imparted to his stories a realism that otherwise might have been difficult to attain.

Simultaneously, under his pseudonyms, Heinlein produced stories which did not fit into his future history.

The entry of the United States into World War II temporarily halted his writing career. He spent the war years in the Naval Experimental Station at Philadelphia, engaged in aviation engineering.

With the end of the war he returned to writing, immediately hitting his stride. In rapid succession he sold to *Collier's, Elk's Magazine, Argosy, Saturday Evening Post,* Standard Magazines, Popular Publications and others. He appeared in two major science fiction anthologies, and he has two books listed for early publication, with others to follow. *Scribner's* will publish his "Rocket Ship Galileo" in Autumn, 1947, and *Fantasy Press* will issue "Beyond This Horizon" early in 1948.

Robert A. Heinlein's contribution to this symposium is an especially appropriate beginning for the series. Within the space of a few thousand words he has offered so many important basic suggestions on the writing of better quality science fiction, that the reader will do well to digest every paragraph. Though intended primarily for the writing of "speculative" fiction, to use his own term, the suggestions apply with surprising force to any kind of fiction writing.

Heinlein's ideas carry additional weight because he is the first of the popular science fiction writers to sell science fiction consistently to the "slicks". Others will follow his lead; and it may well be that this brief article will be the spark that will fire the creative urge in other writers, who will aim for—and hit—the big pay, general fiction magazines.

ON THE WRITING OF SPECULATIVE FICTION

"There are nine-and-sixty ways
Of constructing tribal lays
And every single one of them is right!"
—RUDYARD KIPLING

THERE are at least two principal ways to write speculative fiction — write about people, or write about gadgets. There are other ways; consider Stapleton's "Last and First Men," recall S. Fowler Wright's "The World Below." But the gadget story and the human-interest story comprise most of the field. Most science fiction stories are a mixture of the two types, but we will speak as if they were distinct—at which point I will chuck the gadget story aside, dust off my hands, and confine myself to the human-interest story, that being the sort of story I myself write. I have nothing against the gadget story—I read it and enjoy it—it's just not my pidgin. I am told that this is a how-to-do-it symposium; I'll stick to what I know how to do.

The editor suggested that I write on "Science Fiction in the Slicks". I shan't do so because it is not a separate subject. Several years ago Will F. Jenkins said to me, "I'll let you in on a secret, Bob. *Any* story—science fiction, or otherwise—if it is well written, can be sold to the slicks." Will himself has proved this, so have many other writers—Wylie, Wells, Cloete, Doyle, Ertz, Noyes, many others. You may protest that these writers were able to sell science fiction to the high-pay markets because they were already well-known writers. It just ain't so, pal; on the contrary they are well-known writers because they are skilled at their trade. When they have a science fiction story to write, they turn out a well-written story and it sells to a high-pay market.

An editor of a successful magazine will bounce a poorly-written story from a "name" writer just as quickly as one from an unknown. Perhaps he will write a long letter of explanation and suggestion, knowing as he does that writers are as touchy as white leghorns, but he will bounce it. At most, prominence of the author's name might decide a borderline case.

A short story stands a much better chance with the slicks if it is not more than 5000 words long. A human-interest story stands a better chance with the slicks than a gadget story, because the human-interest story usually appeals to a wider audience than does a gadget story. But this does not rule out the gadget story. Consider "The Note on Danger B" in a recent *Saturday Evening Post* and Wylie's "The Blunder," which appeared last year in *Collier's*.

Let us consider what a story is and how to write one. (Correction: how *I* write one—remember Mr. Kipling's comment!)

A story is an account which is not necessarily true but which is interesting to read.

There are three main plots for the human interest story: boy-meets-girl, The Little Tailor, and the man-who-learned-better. Credit the last category to L. Ron Hubbard; I had thought for years that there were but two plots—he pointed out to me the third type.

Boy-meets-girl needs no definition. But don't disparage it. It reaches from the "Illiad" to John Taine's "Time Stream." It's the greatest story of them all and has never been sufficiently exploited in science fiction. To be sure, it appears in most s-f stories, but how often is it dragged in by the hair and how often is it the compelling and necessary element which creates and then solves the problem? It has great variety: boy-fails-to-meet-girl, boy-meets-girl-too-late, boy-meets-too-many-girls, boy-loses-girl, boy-and-girl-renounce-love-for-higher-purpose. Not science fiction? Here is a

ON THE WRITING OF SPECULATIVE FICTION

throw-away plot; you can have it free: Elderly man meets very young girl; they discover that they are perfectly adapted to each other, perfectly in love, "soul mates". (Don't ask me how. It's up to you to make the thesis credible. If I'm going to have to write this story, I want to be paid for it.)

Now to make it a science fiction story. Time travel? Okay, what time theory—probable-times, classic theory, or what? Rejuvenation? Is this mating necessary to some greater end? Or vice versa? Or will you transcend the circumstances, as C. L. Moore did in that tragic masterpiece "Bright Illusion"?

I've used it twice as tragedy and shall probably use it again. Go ahead and use it yourself. I did not invent it; it is a great story which has been kicking around for centuries.

The "Little Tailor"—this is an omnibus for all stories about the little guy who becomes a big shot, or vice versa. The tag is from the fairy story. Examples: "Dick Whittington," all the Alger books, "Little Caesar," "Galactic Patrol" (but not "Grey Lensman"), "Mein Kampf," David in the Old Testament. It is the Success story, or, in reverse, the story of tragic failure.

The man-who-learned-better; just what it sounds like—the story of a man who has one opinion, point of view, or evaluation at the beginning of the story, then acquires a new opinion or evaluation as a result of having his nose rubbed in some harsh facts. I had been writing this story for years before Hubbard pointed out to me the structure of it. Examples: my "Universe" and "Logic of Empire," Jack London's "South of the Slot," Dickens' "A Christmas Carol."

The definition of a story as something interesting-but-not-necessarily-true is general enough to cover all writers, all stories—even James Joyce, if you find his stuff interesting. (I don't!) For me, a story of the sort I want to write is still further limited to this recipe: a man finds himself in circumstances which create a problem for him. In coping with this problem, the man is changed in some fashion inside himself. The story is over when the inner change is complete—the external incidents may go on indefinitely.

People changing under stress:
A lonely rich man learns comradeship in a hobo jungle.
A milquetoast gets pushed too far and learns to fight.
A strong man is crippled and has to adjust to it.
A gossip learns to hold her tongue.
A hard-boiled materialist gets acquainted with a ghost.
A shrew is tamed.

This is the story of character, rather than incident. It's not everybody's dish, but for me it has more interest than the most overwhelming pure adventure story. It need not be unadventurous; the stress which produces the change in character can be wildly adventurous, and often is.

But what has all this to do with science fiction? A great deal! Much so-called science fiction is not about human beings and their problems, consisting instead of a fictionized framework, peopled by cardboard figures, on which is hung an essay about the Glorious Future of Technology. With due respect to Mr. Bellamy, "Looking Backward" is a perfect example of the fictionized essay. I've done it myself; "Solution Unsatisfactory" is a fictionized essay, written as such. Knowing that it would have to compete with real *story*, I used every device I could think of, some of them hardly admissible, to make it look like a story.

Another type of fiction alleged to be science fiction is the story laid in the future, or on another planet, or in another dimension, or sich, which could just as well have happened on Fifth Avenue, in 1947. Change the costumes back to now, cut out the pseudo-scientific double-talk and the blaster guns and it turns out to be straight adventure story, suitable, with appropriate facelifting, to any other pulp magazine on the news stand.

There is another type of honest-to-goodness science fiction story which is not usually regarded as science fiction: the story of people dealing with contemporary science or technology. We do not ordinarily mean this sort of story when we say "science fiction"; what we do mean is the speculative story, the story embodying the notion "Just suppose—", or "What would happen if—". In the speculative science fiction story accepted science and established facts are extrapolated to produce a new situation, a new framework for human action. As a result of this new situation, new *human* problems are created—and our story is about how human beings cope with those new problems.

The story is *not* about the new situation; it is about coping with problems arising out of the new situation.

Let's gather up the bits and define the Simon-pure science fiction story:

1. The conditions must be, in some respect, different from here-and-now, although the difference may lie only in an invention made in the course of the story.
2. The new conditions must be an essential part of the story.
3. The problem itself — the "plot" — must be a *human* problem.
4. The human problem must be one which is created by, or indispensably affected by, the new conditions.
5. And lastly, no established fact shall be violated, and, furthermore, when the story requires that a theory contrary to present accepted theory be used, the new theory should be rendered reasonably plausible and it must include and explain established facts as satisfactorily as the one the author saw fit to junk. It may be far-fetched, it may seem fantastic, but it must *not* be at variance with observed facts, i.e., if you are going to assume that the human race descended from Martians, then you've *got* to explain our apparent close relationship to terrestrial anthropoid apes as well.

Pardon me if I go on about this. I love to read science fiction, but violation of that last requirement gets me riled. Rocketships should not make banked turns on empty space the way airplanes bank their turns on air. Lizards can't cross-breed with humans. The term "space warp" does not mean anything without elaborate explanation.

Not everybody talking about heaven is going there—and there are a lot of people trying to write science fiction who haven't bothered to learn anything about science. Nor is there any excuse for them in these days of public libraries. You owe it to your readers (a) to bone up on the field of science you intend to introduce into your story (b) unless you yourself are well-versed in that field, you should also persuade some expert in that field to read your story and criticize it before you offer it to an unsuspecting public. Unless you are willing to take this much trouble, please, *please* stick to a contemporary background you are familiar with. Paderewski had to practice; Sonja Henie still works on her school figures; a doctor puts in many weary years before they will let him operate—why should you be exempt from preparatory effort?

The Simon-pure science fiction story — examples of human problems arising out of extrapolations of present science:

Biological warfare ruins the farm lands of the United States; how is Joe Doakes, a used-car dealer, to feed his family?

Interplanetary travel puts us in contact with a race able to read our thoughts; is the testimony of such beings admissible as evidence in a murder trial?

Men reach the Moon; what is the attitude of the Security Council of the United Nations. (Watch out for this one—and hold on to your hats!)

A complete technique for ectogenesis is developed; what is the effect on home, family, morals, religion? (Aldous Huxley left lots of this field unplowed—help yourself.)

And so on. I've limited myself to *my* notions about science fiction, but don't forget Mr. Kipling's comment. In any case it isn't necessary to know how—just go ahead and do it. Write what you like to read. If you have a yen for it, if you get a kick out of "Just imagine—", if you love to

ON THE WRITING OF SPECULATIVE FICTION

think up new worlds, then come on in, the water's fine and there is plenty of room.

But don't write to me to point out how I have violated my own rules in this story or that. I've violated all of them and I would much rather try a new story than defend an old one.

I'm told that these articles are supposed to be some use to the reader. I have a guilty feeling that all of the above may have been more for my amusement than for your edification. Therefore I shall chuck in as a bonus a group of practical, tested rules which, if followed meticulously, will prove rewarding to any writer.

I shall assume that you can type, that you know the accepted commercial format or can be trusted to look it up and follow it, and that you always use new ribbons and clean type. Also, that you can spell and punctuate and can use grammar well enough to get by. These things are merely the word-carpenter's sharp tools. He must add to them these business habits:

1. You must *write*.
2. You must *finish* what you start.
3. You must refrain from rewriting except to editorial order.
4. You must put it on the market.
5. You must keep it on the market until sold.

The above five rules really have more to do with how to write speculative fiction than anything said above them. But they are amazingly hard to follow—which is why there are so few profesisonal writers and so many aspirants, and which is why I am not afraid to give away the racket! But, if you will follow them, it matters not how you write, you will find some editor somewhere, sometime, so unwary or so desperate for copy as to buy the worst old dog you, or I, or anybody else, can throw at him.

WRITING A SCIENCE NOVEL
By John Taine

Editor's Preface

JOHN TAINE

JOHN TAINE, famous for his science novels ever since his Tibetan romance, "The Purple Sapphire", was published in 1924, is the prominent research mathematician, Dr. Eric Temple Bell. Under his own name he has had published a number of popular books on what he describes as "the less inhuman aspects of mathematics and science, for example, mathematicians". These include "Men of Mathematics", "Queen of the Sciences", "The Magic of Numbers", and others. In addition he has written several books, as well as more than two hundred thirty papers, on purely technical mathematics.

He was born in Peterhead, Scotland, on February 7, 1883. After attending various schools in England, he came to the United States (of which he is a naturalized citizen) in 1902, entering Stanford University in the fall of 1902, and graduating in 1904. There he specialized in mathematics, and in 1907 was a teaching fellow at the University of Washington, where he took his Master's degree. In the academic year 1911-12 he attended Columbia University, taking his doctor's degree in mathematics.

Since 1926 he has been Professor of Mathematics at California Institute of Technology. He is a member of the

American Association for the Advancement of Science, the American Mathematical Society, the Mathematical Association of America (of which he is past-president), Circolo Matematico di Palermo, the Calcutta Mathematical Society, and the National Academy of Science.

Dr. Bell devotes most of his time to mathematics, teaching and research. Science fiction is one of his hobbies; research in mathematics leaves little time for fiction writing. Despite this, John Taine has appeared as author of thirteen published science novels, and has written several others which have not yet seen print. His most recent science novel is "The Forbidden Garden", published by *Fantasy Press*.

John Taine's work is distinctive for its originality and plausibility. His concepts and their developments are his own; and even his wildest flights of imagination are convincing. This believable quality, inherent in his work, is due in part to his gripping portrayal of natural phenomena—the disintegration of a tremendous frozen waterfall in "The Forbidden Garden", or the series of cataclysmic earthquakes and volcanic eruptions in "The Iron Star", for example. Then, too, the characters in his stories are real people, and his science, as would be expected, is always sound.

In his contribution to this symposium, John Taine has devoted considerable thought to a phase of science fiction writing which has received little attention from the other authors in the series. This is the matter of research for material, and the acquiring of a sound scientific story background. Since this is basic in every type of science fiction writing, and since so much of Taine's article may be applied similarly to the writing of short stories or novelettes, it has been placed second in the series.

In addition, John Taine describes a unique method of developing new ideas for science fiction. This device, if followed consistently, should furnish the writer with a steady supply of original story backgrounds. Again, though Taine mentions it as a method of developing plots for science novels, it will be equally useful for shorter material.

WRITING A SCIENCE NOVEL

IN a certain tavern in Pasadena there is a motto over the bar to the effect that neither Liquor, nor Wealth, nor Education ever made a fool of any man; they merely provide a Born Damned Fool with a wider stage for his foolishness. Having seen a great deal of Education, I can certify the correctness of the motto in that one respect.

In science fiction a trio to be watched with care is Knowledge, Education, and Consistency. A moderate amount of each of the first two is necessary for the writing of a readable science novel. A deliberate parade of either is literary misconduct as offensive as the complementary misdemeanor of insulting your reader by "writing down" to meet his supposed ignorance. The art, or the trick if you prefer, is not to take whatever knowledge and education you may have too seriously. If you must be pedantic and cram everything you know into your intended fiction, you may find yourself with a stodgy treatise on neurospora or nuclear physics on your hands. As for consistency, that also should not be obtruded or overdone. But without some logic to cement it, the story falls apart.

We shall consider each of the dangerous three in turn, Knowledge first. It was remarked long ago by a woman writer on science (Mary Somerville) that the amount of knowledge necessary for making an original contribution to science is many times as great as that which suffices for an intelligent reading and appreciation of even the more difficult scientific masterpieces. The like is true in science fiction. The writer must know considerably more about the scientific matrix of his story than can be expected from those sensible people who read for entertainment. Further, he must know it so well that he can present it incidentally and so effectively that the reader does not have to use an unabridged dictionary and the latest encyclopaedia to follow the essential thread. A great French mathematician (d'Alembert) asserted that no mathematician has really understood his own work until he can go out into the street and explain it satisfactorily to the first man he meets. That, of course, is a counsel of perfection.

On the practical, attainable level, an accurate knowledge of the science underlying a story will enable the writer to ignore those technical details that can be disregarded without making nonsense of the scientific foundation. Stories based on nonsense collapse, burying the writer. For if the writer has not a competent mastery of his scientific materials, his story will be ripped apart by at least some of his younger readers. They take their science fiction seriously, and do not enjoy having their intelligence outraged by incompetence. Another reason, equally important, for more knowledge of a particular science than is actually worked into a story will be noted near the end of this article. For the moment we must see how the necessary knowledge may be gained.

So far as fiction is concerned, scientific knowledge is of two kinds, dead and living, or fossil and active. Fossil science is not suitable for scientific fiction. Vast deposits of it lie buried in the histories of science, the schoolbooks, the college texts, and the encyclopaedias. It is not all wrong; it is not all useless; it is merely dead for the purposes of romance. Much of it must be assimilated by anyone who wishes to get on to the kind of science that can be profitably mined for stories.

About two hundred years ago an exciting fiction could have been based on the two-fluid theory of electricity. Today, even a professor of the humanities would know better than to attempt anything livelier than a historical monograph on that ingenious but long-defunct theory. Human nature, especially as portrayed in the novel of manners and character, may not change much with the years; science does. It is not a question here of building a story round the newest gadget or the latest fad in speculation. It is simply the common-sense precaution of avoiding moth-eaten antiques and wormy ideas. What is sound in the older science was exploited long since, and the readers of science fiction are as tired of it as are the scientists themselves. But how is the prospective writer to find his way into living science, and how is he to see what to do when he gets there?

Well, so far as I know, there are no shortcuts. There is only one road. As Rossetti said in regard to composing a poem, a certain amount of fundamental brainwork is necessary. That, and that alone, will lead anyone out of the fossil age into the scientific present. Having arrived in this parplexing time, what is the would-be writer to do next? The answer is immediate: use his imagination.

Unless a writer has an exceptionally vivid imagination, science fiction is no field for him. The ability to visualize sharply and steadily is one evidence of the right type of imagination for this kind of writing. Probably it is inborn, but it can be intensified by conscious effort. Scenes in full color with all the movements the writer describes are presented to his inner vision as if he were watching a real action being played out before him. He has only to report what he sees. When the story is well on its way it develops of itself, and the teller is sometimes surprised at what he sees but did not knowingly anticipate.

Assuming that the writer is not petrified by brainwork and has some imagination, we must see what sort of work he should expect to do. Only one or two details can be noted. He must read scientific books, many of them, some of them quite hard, others rather dull. Some will be the standard texts for up-to-date schools and colleges. With the help of somebody who knows something about science, not necessarily a professional teacher, he will soon learn what to skim and what to linger over till it is his. All this is for the older, basic things without which vital, fictionable science is gibberish to writer and reader alike. The workable ideas for stories are in the last few chapters of the more recent books.

It is wise to glance at the date of publication of any book on science. If the book is more than ten years old (two to five in some of the physical sciences), it had probably better be put back on the shelf. Even the best of the standard texts contain little that is sufficiently alive to be immediately useful or suggestive for fiction. Nor does yesterday's or today's newspaper offer much, if anything at all. Most of the science reported in journalism is either trite or out of date before it is printed. I am not trying to make all this seem harder than it need be or is. But to produce a story that will stimulate an active imagination, a personal familiarity with some science that is not already embalmed in the text books or indecently buried in the newspaper seems to be essential. Where and how is it to be acquired?

It may be assumed that the prospective writer of a science novel has had at least an elementary course in science at school, or that he has had enough interest in science to get up some of it by himself. The more fortunate will have gone on to college, specializing in science. These will know how to proceed, and need no advice. Likewise for graduate students in science, a surprisingly large number of whom read science fiction. Nor do the men who make their livings at science and write an occasional story for the fun of it, or to finance an addition to the doghouse, need to be told anything. The one who needs guidance is the scientifically untrained writer with a creative imagination and the will to break into a comparatively new kind of fiction. This one may be saved time, money and trouble by attending to a few simple hints, gathered from the experience of practising writers.

Whoever hopes to find promising leads for unhackneyed stories in the science department of the average good public library is likely to be disappointed. The scientific periodicals, so-called, to which public libraries in all but the largest cities

WRITING A SCIENCE NOVEL

subscribe, are not those in which scientists report and discuss current progress in science, and by "current" I mean less than ten years old. The professional journals, of which there are a great many, are probably too special to be of much help, although an alert prospector can often pick up nuggets he would not come across elsewhere in the most forbidding wilderness of technicalities. But these journals are accessible, as a rule, only in university libraries, and not always there in the more backward States. If there is a good university library within reach, it should be visited regularly. It will take time to find one's way about; but the habit of consulting current scientific literature, once formed, is hard to shake off and quickly makes the task of keeping abreast of progress easy and enjoyable.

Suppose, however, there is not a decent scientific library within a hundred miles. What then? There are the popular and semipopular scientific periodicals, both weeklies and monthlies. It is humiliating for an American to be forced to admit that there is not a single periodical of this kind published in the United States that is worth its subscription price. This is not a personal crotchet. Its factual truth can be checked by asking any scientific man in the country who is not completely ossified. The two or three specimens with the largest circulations are insults to American science and cynical concessions to the scientific inadequacy of general American education. The dreary stuff they print is for the most part trivial and boring. Fortunately few prospective students of science ever look at them, and working men of science who subscribe to these wretched things "for the good of the cause", usually file them in the wastebasket.

Intelligent scientific journalism is one of the things in which we do not excel. The Europeans know how to do it, and have been doing it for a long time. To keep up with what is happening in science, one or other of the better foreign weekly or monthly general scientific periodicals should be inspected regularly. Few of the articles, especially at first, will be of interest or profit to the prospector. But those few will pay for everything.

To appreciate this, imagine what might have happened to science novels if Jules Verne had chanced on the really new and potentially revolutionary science of his time. In the 1860's Clerk Maxwell's mathematical prediction of wireless waves was current. Verne was then in his thirties. In 1887 Hertz produced wireless waves in his laboratory. In the 1890's television was accurately forecast in reasonable detail by a prominent English electrical engineer. All that deterred him, he said, from realizing his forecast was the colossal expense. Verne at the time was still active. When these things were new, they offered as imaginative a mind as Verne's an opportunity to surpass the Arabian Nights. Yet Verne, to whom they were accessible had he looked in the right places, missed them. Doubtless science fictionists are overlooking equally good leads today.

It would hardly be proper here to advertise by name any of these foreign periodicals which the writer of science fiction will do well to inspect at least once a month. The best of all is an English weekly, quite expensive but worth its price. Those who can read German will find the corresponding periodical in that language worth their frequent attention. Any competent reference librarian will know these two. The English one may be found in some public libraries in the larger cities, also in the reading rooms of universities with any pretensions to being educational institutions rather than athletic clubs and finishing schools. New York, of course, has nearly everything, including librarians who know their profession.

In addition to books and periodicals, there used to be, and may still be for all I know, excellent popular lecture courses on current science given by the scientific staffs of the colleges and universities. These were open to the public without charge. Doubtless more such lectures would be offered if there were a concerted request for them. The prospective writer of science fiction who is not too proud to attend lectures by men who know what they are talking about, may find that it is possible, occasionally, to learn something even from a professor of physics. I once knew a man who astonished himself by learning something from a pure mathematician, and getting not only a good story out of the experience, but also an ingenious tactic for constructing any number of stories. It had nothing to do with the late Monsieur Polti's somewhat mystical recipes for writing.

Before passing on to Education, the real devil of the dangerous three, we must note a possible pitfall. I believe that only the man with exceptional opportunities and corresponding natural endowments can hope to do satisfactory fiction in both the physical and the biological sciences, or in either of these and the engineering sciences. The last presupposes an acquaintance with some physics and chemistry. H. G. Wells had the necessary education for the first two, and his curiosity and imagination sufficed for the third. But Wells was a genius; and although some of the present generation complain that his tempo is too slow, his mastery of his scientific materials is undisputed, and even those of his stories that are outdated still make sense. Less gifted aspirants will probably get the most out of their talents if they invest all they have in just one of the physical, the biological, and the engineering sciences. This does not imply that a mixture of two, or even of all three, in a story will result in a general mess. The mixing must be done with skill and caution, and the particular one of the three in which the writer is most proficient should dominate the theme. A man who is at home in physics but all abroad in biology can make some terrible mistakes when he attempts a story based on the genetics of oysters.

It might be thought that all this study of science is ample education for anyone who wishes to write a science novel. Unfortunately for the prospective writer it is only part of the necessary foundation. The rest is education in the narrow sense of learning how to write a story that people will read. How this is to be accomplished, I have not the slightest idea. The urge to write is neither sufficient nor necessary. Many say they want to write but never do. Others detest writing and yet have writing saddled on them by editors with a flair for picking winners.

Nearly all universities in the country and many high schools and junior colleges offer courses in writing for money, if not for pleasure. Never having had any firsthand experience of such courses, I can only pass on what my writing friends tell me. The reports are spotty. Some schools have graduated brilliantly successful writers; but whether the school training was responsible for the successes, it is impossible to check scientifically. There seems to be a concensus that the technique of the short story can be taught, and that it is taught well in the better institutions, both public and private. There may be something in this, as all but a conspicuous few short stories now being turned out look very much alike, according to the critics.

As for the teachers, it is curious but true that the best teachers of writing are but seldom writers of note themselves. Perhaps after all this is not so strange. Great musical performers have been trained by men who could never have made a public reputation for themselves. So whoever may be inclined to disparage teachers of writing because they themselves don't write, should have enough scientific objectivity to find out whether the nearest teacher can be of any help to him.

For novels and longer stories not much seems to be offered, and the writer must develop his instincts for structure himself. An elementary device that often works is to imagine a dramatic climax and develop the story steadily toward it. The climax in a science novel will usually be determined automatically by the science round which the story is constructed, less frequently by the characters.

There is one thing that the newcomer to science fiction should realize and appreciate. The science fiction novel and the science story have graduated from the kindergarten. A good story sloppily written will find little favor with the

WRITING A SCIENCE NOVEL

fans. Although the science fiction devotee may not be able to run down what it is that annoys him in an otherwise good yarn, probably it is bad writing. Competent presentation is the rule, not the exception, today. As in the acquisition of the necessary scientific knowledge, so here. A greater familiarity with decent writing than is evident to the reader should be part of the writer's equipment. Otherwise, his story is likely to date itself in the dark ages of science fiction, when any crackpot with a sufficiently crazy idea could work it up into an impossible story, execrably written, and sell it to an editor of little discrimination and less taste. According to many successful writers the best way to write respectably is to read the works of men who write better than respectably.

Granted that the writer has mastered the rudiments of writing, what should he write about in a science novel? Obviously, science. But of itself science is not enough. The impact of science on the emotions and actions of human beings is usually demanded by the reader. Few readers any longer can work themselves into a lather over the shattering collisions of brainless supergadgets. All that sort of thing, if done consistently, gets no farther than Newton's third law of motion. Personally, I should like to see a gadgetless story with the human element reduced almost to zero. It could be done.

Assuming that human beings, appropriately disposed, enhance the beauties and wonders of the scientific scene (a doubtful assumption), we land at once in unsettled controversies. What, for example, about a love interest? Well, what about it? Young readers are capable of saying the heck with it. More mature addicts of novels in the classical tradition may feel cheated unless they bite into a thick slice of billing and cooing, mustarded perhaps with a dab or two of fornication or adultery, solidly embedded in the scientific sandwich. The adult appetite for these old staples is insatiable. But are they palatable when slipped into a novel of science? Certainly not always.

OF WORLDS BEYOND

If there is some logical (or biological) reason why a luscious heroine should display her charms in a science novel, she does not have to be lugged in by the hair. She will enter by herself, usually uninvited by the writer and sometimes to his exasperation. As a general rule, love interest in a scientific fiction is a red herring to bewilder the reader and turn him off a trail that should, but does not, lead straight from the beginning to the end of the story. If there is not sufficient sexless interest in the story to hold the reader's attention, no fortuitous blonde is going to lure him on to the last page. Yet many a misguided writer has got not only himself but his stories all fouled up with superfluous women.

For example, there have been numerous variants in scientific fiction of that corny classic of Adam and Eve adrift on a raft in a tropical sea, like two sizzling eggs in a pan of hot grease. However thick the scientific haze surrounding the raft, the shapely pair on it are still clearly recognizable as the progenitors of a race of stupids as dumb as themselves to succeed those who were chased out of some Eden, or who drowned when their ship went down, or who blew up their civilization with atomic bombs. The scientific disguises of this protean classic add nothing but confusion and spinach to the corn. Any reader above the juvenile moron level knows what is going to happen and, if he is interested, he wants to see it happen in the classic way without any scientific monkey business. So, if he has any sense at all, he takes the book back to the library and draws out any one of several hundred that will give him the real thing in all its virginal impurity.

Science fiction is one of the places where a pretty girl can be a damned nuisance. Conversely, almost any type of scientific fiction is no peg on which to hang a love story. A sexy story larded over with science is something quite different from a science novel based on sex. Here the possibilities are limitless. Not to raise any unjustified hopes, I may remind conclusion-jumpers that sex does not have to be pinned onto human beings exclusively. Tadpoles will do, salamanders are excellent. This field has been little cultivated by the writers of scientific fiction.

Passing on to the third member of the dangerous three, Consistency, I need say little about it, as Mr. Williamson is discussing the logic of fantasy in this series. There is however one prolific source of new science stories that may be overlooked unless it is pointed out, as it is a technique of those least scientific of all scientists, the mathematicians. They have been using it for over a century with remarkable success in the invention of new things. A simple example from the multiplication table will bring out the gist.

If we multiply one number by another, say 7 by 8, we get the same result, 56, as if we multiply these numbers in the reverse order, 8 by 7. For thousands of years it was tacitly assumed that, in order to get a *consistent* arithmetic, it is *necessary* (not merely *sufficient*) to *assume* that the results of multiplying any two numbers together are *the same* for *both orders* in which the mutiplication is performed. Is it possible to drop the assumption and to imagine or invent a new kind of 'numbers' for which the order of multiplication gives *different* results?

One way of attempting to settle such a question is to *assume* that the answer is 'yes', and then to develop the logical consequences of this assumption. If no contradiction is encountered, the hopeful investigator looks about for some mathematical example, or some physical phenomenon, which he knows hangs together consistently, and tries to interpret his new system in terms of the example or the phenomenon. If he succeeds, he is justified in assuming that his new system is consistent. He then proceeds to develop its logical consequences as far as he can. In this way he creates a mathematical science that had not been imagined before he produced it. In the case of common multiplication, the new numbers and their 'arithmetic' (more properly 'algebra') found their ready interpretation in physics, first in the mechanics of rotation, then in optics and elsewhere. What was strange a century ago is now a commonplace to undergraduates in the physical and engineering sciences.

To apply this technique to the production of science fiction, we first make as complete a list as we can of all the assumptions on which a particular connected piece of science is based. Then we see what would happen if one of these assumptions were either ignored or contradicted—these are not logically equivalent, as may be readily seen. We then go ahead with our mutilated piece of science and try to imagine what might happen in a world where such a science actually described what could be observed. Instead of ignoring or contradicting one of the assumptions outright, we may modify it slightly, say by relaxing its stringency, and develop the consequences as before. What has just been described can be applied in a similar manner to two or more of the assumptions of a science, or to several sciences.

At any stage we may allow ourselves some latitude if the logic gets too cramping for comfort. But if we have made a lucky start by picking the right assumption to ignore, or to contradict, or to modify, we shall squeeze through and come out with a convincing story. If anyone gets through merely by ingenious wriggling without tampering anywhere with the restraints, he may astound himself with a major scientific discovery. Einstein did just that.

One example will have to suffice. It is a basic assumpton of the special theory of relativity that no body, say a spaceship, can move with a speed greater than that of light. To assume the contrary, and have the ship outspeeding light, would blow up the ship and probably the universe. This is a disaster of the first magnitude for a writer who must transport his hero to the nearest spiral nebula in forty eight hours to head off a threatened invasion by the Andromedans. But everything would work out perfectly if the awkward assumption were denied. So the science fictionist consigns the assumption to the physicists and blazes whooping on his way through interstellar space. Such stories have been written. In the present state of science they are impossibilities.

WRITING A SCIENCE NOVEL

Yet, if skillfully done, they can be made quite convincing.

Anyone who commits this particular scientific mayhem (I was deliberately guilty myself once years ago), has a defense, though a weak one. The assumption about the limiting speed of moving bodies is after all an assumption, and is recognized as such in reputable science. All the evidence to date confirms its reasonableness if not its absolute, hundred-per-cent truth. Billions of years hence the physical universe may have evolved into another in which it will no longer be convenient to retain the cramping assumption. In short, it may not be a necessity everywhere and for all time, world without end, Amen.

Less profane tampering with the hypotheses of science is safer and leads to consequences spectacular enough for the most avid devourer of science fiction. Thus some astrophysicists are beginning to doubt the universality of the second law of thermodynamics. To deny the universal validity of this law in order to concoct a good story need not, therefore, offend anyone but an over-stuffed pedant. In this mathematical or logical device of tampering with the assumptions we have the most cogent reason for a writer of science fiction to know much more science than he works into his stories.

In conclusion, it seems obvious that H. G. Wells got some of his best effects by using this device. He may not always have used it consciously. He was an adept. He also is a prize exhibit of what a man can do in science fiction if he keeps up with a constantly growing science. If you have never read "Men Like Gods", get it out of the library and study it in the light of your knowledge of what happened at Alamogordo, Hiroshima, Nagasaki, and Bikkini. No mucker picking over the refuse of obsolete science could have written that book. Wells got his key idea from what at the time was the almost exclusive knowledge of Rutherford and his associates. It was not in any book on any library shelf. And if you are interested in knowing where Wells got his clowning villain, it was from unsympathetic observation of Mr. Winston Churchill. Then, if you think Wells came down a little too hard on his victim, observe how close he came to describing the current reactions of politicians, statesmen, and the military to the appalling facts of atomic energy, for which nothing in their antiquated education or their retarded mentalities has prepared them. And last, recall that it was an eminent atomic physicist, and not the science fictionist Wells, who kept assuring the world that human beings would never get enough energy out of atoms to blow the whistle on a peanut stand.

Now that I have tried to tell you how to do it, you may ask why I don't do it myself and produce a story that will keep you up all night. Did you ever know a physician who was competent to prescribe for his own ailments?

THE LOGIC OF FANTASY
By Jack Williamson

Editor's Preface

JACK WILLIAMSON

THE CAREER of Jack Williamson began in the mining town of Bisbee, in what was then Arizona Territory, on April 29, 1908. A pioneering tendency in his parents had turned them from teaching school to cattle ranching. The family lived on a mountainous Sonora ranch until the Mexican revolution of 1910, and then after a few years on an unsuccessful irrigation project near Pecos, Texas, migrated by covered wagon to a lonely homestead on the Llano Estacado of New Mexico, where his parents and brother are still in the cattle business.

Taught to read at home, Williamson first met science through the physics texts and an old two-volume encyclopedia in the battered trunk that held his father's library. He attended grade school only two years—riding to school behind his father's saddle and suffering the social calamity of being teacher's boy—and graduated from a country high school in 1925.

Williamson's discovery of the pioneer science fiction magazine, the old Gernsback "Amazing Stories", in 1926, was, in his own words, "a supreme adventure", opening to him a fabulous new frontier. Vaguely, prior to this discovery, he had planned to be some sort of scientist. Now he knew he must write science fiction.

He made his first sale in 1928 after two years of spare-time effort. Working at night, by the smoky light of a kerosene lamp, pounding an antique typewriter that had a faded purple ribbon, he had turned out four or five rejected epics—and then "The Metal Man" was published without his having been informed of its acceptance!

He entered college that fall at Canyon, Texas, and later attended New Mexico University, majoring in chemistry and psychology. Keeping a little house on the ranch as permanent headquarters, he has lived in American cities ranging from Santa Fe and Key West to Los Angles and New York, writing and studying. During the recent war he served in the South Pacific.

Williamson has sold more than a million and a half words of fantasy and science fiction, appearing consistently in every major publication in his chosen field. With the recent publication of his "The Legion of Space" in book form, *Fantasy Press* has made Williamson's work available to a new and highly appreciative body of readers.

In his contribution to this symposium of articles, Jack Williamson has presented in clear, concise language some of the basic principles involved in the production of good fantasy and science fiction. Not new ideas, perhaps—rather, he has given concrete form to fundamental truths half-realized by successful writers and of inestimable value to beginners in the field. He offers no foolproof mechanical device for the mass production of salable fiction and an unbroken flow of publishers' checks; but he does point out some of the barriers which interrupt that flow, and indicates a safe course around them.

Logic—in no other field of fiction writing is it more important than in that of science-fantasy. Upon it depends that most elusive quality, verisimilitude, which makes a story convincing. Upon it, too, hinges the willingness of the reader to suspend normal disbelief, and to accompany the writer on his flight of fancy.

THE LOGIC OF FANTASY

Even the sky isn't the limit—not in fantasy. Anything can happen. A man may find himself transformed into a werewolf, in a tale of the uncanny, or even into a werepterodactyl. A science fiction hero can fly an ordinary airplane all the way to Mars. Anything goes—

Or does it?

Actually, the fantasy field does give the writer a great deal of freedom. He can explore the past to the dawn of time, and the expanding universe to anything he wants to imagine, and the future until all wonders happen. Yet that freedom has it limits; fantastic fiction is bound by certain definite rules of logic.

There are, I think, two basic principles, arising from human psychology, which can help any writer turn his raw material of memories and emotions into soundly built, moving, and successful stories. Doubtless most writers follow them unconsciously. However, I feel that a conscious knowledge of craftsmanship is often useful in selecting and shaping material for a fantasy—or for any other kind of story.

The first principle, which we may call the logic of premise, requires that the reader should be asked, in any one story, to assume only a single basic premise. H. G. Wells states that principle in the introduction to his "Seven Famous Novels," and the novels themselves show that he applied it deliberately and brilliantly.

A fuller analysis of writing problems, however, will show that this logic of premise alone is not enough. On a different level, the writer must also regard the logic of character—as Wells of course did. The first is an aid to unity; the second to real coherence and the emphasis of drama.

Conscious application of these two principles gives the plotting of a fantasy story something of the same orderly precision involved in demonstrating a mathematical theorem. There is the same pleasure in a successful demonstration—plus the hope of a publisher's check!

Both these principles are determined by the psychology of the reader—who must always be considered, because writing is communication, and any kind of communication is a matter of a successful technique with which to reach and move some audience.

The reader begins a story with an open mind. He wants amusement, and he's willing to grant any necessary premise, just to get things going. He will cheerfully agree—if he's in the mood for fantasy—that the perfect robot has at last been invented, or that your heroine can murder a man with witchcraft.

But one assumption is enough. Two would wreck the story's unity. The reader demands internal consistency. He requires that everything in the story shall be—or seem to be—a logical consequence of what has gone before. The logic of fiction, however, is fortunately a little less rigid than that of geometry. If sometimes art is needed to give story-logic the ring of truth, then the writer is an artist!

The reader is willing to play the game. He will gladly follow and accept all the complications that come logically from that first premise, so long as his interest is held. But he properly resents anything that breaks the rules.

The more striking the premise, the more strict is the logical discipline required to present it successfully. Writers of ordinary and adventure stories, I suspect, are often able to get away with coincidences and improbabilities which would sadly mar a tale of vampires or interstellar flight.

Incidental marvels should be strictly excluded. The reality and wonder of the one selected premise are best brought out by contrast with background material that is perfectly convincing, sometimes even commonplace.

John W. Campbell's still-grieved-for *Unknown Worlds* was, necessarily, based upon that first principle of fantasy. Analysis of a few *Unknown* stories, I think, will show that each of them stands, or seems to stand, upon a single axiom.

The incidents, for instance, of my own novel, "Darker than You Think," follow from the single proposition that the human race is a hybrid breed. Besides the predominant strain of *homo sapiens,* there is an alien taint of *homo lycanthropus.* The logical consequences and developments of that assumption make the story.

By the laws of genetics, such a mixed breed would produce occasional throwbacks. The reader, having accepted the original proposition, is willing to grant those throwbacks the same powers the original race of wolf-men possessed. To aid the illusion, the setting is placed in a modern American town. Most of the characters are familiar types.

Contrast is always useful. The effect of the strange and unusual can always be intensified, by placing it against the familiar pattern of normal life, in which the people act like those the reader knows.

"Reign of Wizardry," another *Unknown* novel, was written from a suggestion of Mr. Campbell's—that the magicians of the prehistoric Minoan culture actually knew their stuff! The myth of Theseus, in other words, is based on fact. Research in the New York City public library provided abundant material, and all of it I examined against the touchstone of that basic axiom, selecting only what fitted. The sinister and tantalizing mysteries of the vanished sea-kingdom of Crete took on a convincing reality. By the time I settled down, in Sante Fe, to write the story, I felt that wizened, fearful little Snish was actually a master magician.

"Conscience, Limited," an *Unknown* short story, simply postulates Satan and Hell. Not quite a novel assumption—but its logical development leads to more interesting complications. The arrival of modern business men, with their principles of glad-handed service and their high-pressure efficiency methods, has resulted in a reorganization of that hardy and respected institution. The lawyer-hero finds himself a devil's advocate, fitted out with brief case and fountain pen, assigned to get his unholy clients admitted into Heaven.

This logic of premise applies equally to science fiction stories, because science fiction is simply a specialized type of fantasy, in which the prime assumption usually is a new scientific discovery or invention.

Science fiction is doubtless more popular nowadays than fantasy of the supernatural type, because science has become the modern equivalent of magic. Now, when the news is filled with atomic weapons, rocket test flights, and astounding reports of "flying saucers," the threshold of doubt is very low for scientific wonders. Old-style magic is somewhat out of fashion—though doubtless some readers turn gladly to it, just to escape the harassing wonders of the scientific age.

Nothing is impossible. That is the credo of the science fictioneer—and evidently also the working principle of the research technician. Science is crowding very close on the heels of fiction. The average reader will accept any superscientific device whatever as a story-axiom—so long as the logic of premise is reasonably well observed.

The science fiction magazines tempt a wide range of tastes. One chain caters to sheer paranoia. Another magazine is mostly action-adventure, excellently written, with a minimum of heavy science. A third group offers a wide range of more adult material, ranging from ghost stories to highbrow science. A fourth magazine is deliberately edited for technicians, often using heavily scientific stories and articles. And the general magazines, including the "slicks," are beginning to feature fantasy and science fiction.

To consider the logic of premise in a few of my own scientific stories: The opening chapter of "The Legion of Space" reveals that old John Delmar, with a faculty for "remembering" the future, has been writing a history of the next thousand years. Having accepted that, the reader isn't

THE LOGIC OF FANTASY

likely to balk at the logical consequences of a thousand years of history and scientific progress, even though they include space flight and interstellar war.

"The Legion of Time" was based on a slightly more novel premise—in fact, Mr. Campbell announced this story as a "mutant", meaning that its first premise was a bit different from those of previous time-travel stories; and I believe the same theme has since been used in a number of other stories.

Briefly, the premise is this: Future time is not determined, but is merely a matter of probability. (Quantum physics, incidentally, offers support to that.) Time travellers, therefore, don't find themselves in "the" future, but merely in one of several possible futures. But all those futures, in the logic of fiction, can't become real; one possible world must fade away before another can exist. Logically, then, perhaps the hero becomes involved in the battle between two rival possible worlds—and two possible girls—fighting for realization. If either comes to exist, then the other never was.

"Golden Blood," which ran as a serial in *Weird Tales,* was based on the prime fact that, some thousands of years ago, volcanic vapors in a hidden Arabian cave slowly altered the protoplasm of a few living beings exposed to it—a man, a woman, a tiger, and a snake — to change them into still-living, eternal gold. That premise, I think, makes an acceptable foundation for the mystery and adventure of the plot.

A good rule of story construction, by the way, is to make the reader want to know before you tell him. The various consequences of your basic premise may be presented first, as a series of bewildering and astounding riddles. Your hero battles the unknown, until finally he is able to tie all the strands together, and find his triumphant way at last to the hidden premise.

For another example of that, in a novelette called "The Equalizer," my premise was the philosophic idea that the prevailing form of government, in any historic period, depends on the current state of military technology—or, more broadly that social institutions are functions of technical progress. To demonstrate that idea dramatically, I wanted to show how a simple invention causes people to toss aside, overnight, the whole elaborate fabric of what we call civilization. But I felt that the mere narration of that, lacking any essential conflict, could be pretty dull.

As a means of creating suspense, I put the most of my characters on an expedition just returning to Earth, as the story opens, after twenty years in space. They find the great fortress on the Moon abandoned. On Earth, the cities are empty. It is clear that the people have simply walked out, leaving their valuables behind. The characters, naturally, want to know what has happened. That desire motivates the action. By the time they reach the solution, the reader is likely, I hope, to share their desperate interest in the facts and the reasons why.

The logic of premise, I feel, is essential to the soundly constructed fantasy, yet I don't think that it, alone, is enough to assure a unified, emphatic dramatic effect. The whole feeling and attitude of the reader toward the story will be determined by the behavior of the people in it. The reader can hardly be expected to take the wonders and mysteries any more seriously than the characters do.

Everything depends on the sovereign reader and his mood. If he likes the story, and takes a partizan interest in the perplexities and struggles of the characters, he may be absorbed enough to overlook some minor inconsistency. If he's bored or displeased, on the other hand, he'll be alert for any flaw. It is necessary to win the reader fully, and the surest way to do that is through the logic of character.

People are the most important landmarks in this uncertain world. We strive to know them, in life and art, for what they are. We want to know their inward traits—outward appearances, actually, are only useful clues. We expect them to retain their identity, through changing times.

THE LOGIC OF FANTASY

Plot can be defined as simply a logical device for proving character. An individual faces a situation, in fiction or life, and his own nature causes him to respond to it in terms of emotion, purpose, and action. Plot, then, becomes an arrangement of opposing forces, set up to test the strength of that character-reaction. The character is forced to show the kind of man he is. In the ending, the crucible of plot has proved that he is fine metal, or base, or more likely some alloy of the two.

The reader is interested in people. Places and things are important only in the responses people make to them. A scientific gadget is significant only to the extent that the reader can be shown its effect on human beings. An abstract theme has no value until its human meaning is dramatized.

Usually, the major premise of a fantasy is part of the story-situation, to which the characters respond. The significance of it is made clear by showing human beings reacting to it, in feeling and word and purposeful deed. The intensity of interest will depend on the weight of that human impact, on the drama of conflicting purposes.

For this brief analysis, we may define purpose as the distinguishing quality of life. A single-cell paramecium seems to show purpose, when it swims after food. So does a man when he fights an enemy or decides to give up smoking. Purpose is simply the direction of activity, the organized and usually conscious reaction to a whole situation. It arises out of organic needs. It is reinforced by the chemistry of emotion. It impels speech, thought, and action. It leads to achievement or to failure. It is the driving power of life, and the backbone of character.

In the story-opening, the chief character responds to something in terms of purpose—and the plot interest depends greatly on how novel and vital his purpose is. In the body of the narrative, that same purpose impels him to make a series of attempts toward satisfaction. Usually he meets failures which test his motive traits, incidentally stirring his own emotions and the reader's. In the ending, he either wins or fails, and the significant outcome of the test is made clear.

That is the frame of the action story, stated briefly and pretty much in the nomenclature of Dr. John Gallishaw, whose texts on writing show a sound insight into the psychological problems of dramatic craftsmanship. It is basic, because it describes the common pattern of life—the pattern of stimulus and response.

This emphasis on purpose, however, doesn't mean that every character must be a monomaniac. Living beings learn a variety of reactions to various stimuli, many of them incompatible and always conflicting. A penurious man may really love his extravagant wife, and be torn between emotions. Greed may cause a business man to swindle his best friend. Such conflicts of emotion and purpose, solved in action, reveal the truth of character.

That revelation of human beings, through conflict and solution, is the material of all drama. But it must be tailored by the familiar laws of unity, coherence, and emphasis, to fit the human mind. It must be organized by logic, and made significant. Because the reader, in this confusing world, is looking for meaning. In real life, there is very little certainty. The patterns we seek are often shattered into black chaos—there is senseless wrong and merciless disaster and capricious reward. Perhaps that is one reason why so many readers turn to the friendlier world of fiction, where logic prevails and truth remains true.

However that may be, the logic of character provides the writer with a convenient device for winning the sympathetic attention of the reader. If he recognizes the quivering bundle of conflicting traits as a fellow human being, if he understands the purposes of the main character and shares them vicariously, then he's likely, I think, to read on as that character's staunch ally.

"Non-Stop to Mars," a novelette that ran in the old *Argosy*, will serve, I think, as an example of such character-logic as applied to an actual problem in story-building—and

THE LOGIC OF FANTASY

one, perhaps, a little more difficult than common, for the editor remarked after he had bought the story that he would certainly have rejected it in synopsis form, as too improbable.

That improbable and not very new idea was simply a flight to Mars—non-stop, necessarily!—in an ordinary airplane. The most obvious scientific difficulty, of course, is the total lack of air over nearly all the distance. But I've found that such difficulties, in plotting, can frequently be turned to constructive use—difficulties, after all, are the very reagents the writer needs, to set up dramatic tests to prove the traits of his character.

In this case, the flight obviously is going to require some kind of aerial bridge between the planets. That necessity suggests the tube through which Mars is sucking away Earth's atmosphere. And that device, once arrived at, becomes the story's prime fact. No such premise is likely to be enough, however, until the logic of character is also used to win the friendly interest of the reader.

Since this is to be a non-stop flight, what is more logical than to make the hero a man whose business is making spectacular flights? It is perfectly in character for such a man to fly to Mars, yet there is a possible pitfall here. If the hero were portrayed as a selfish exhibitionist, there would be an immediate loss of sympathy. I tried to avoid that by showing that he is merely conducting an out-of-doors advertising service in a business-like way. Other people handle the publicity and benefit from it. Really, the hero is doing a hard and dangerous job, for which he isn't too well paid. These traits are dramatized, again, by introducing a girl who misunderstands them and quarrels with the hero. In the ending, however, she has cause to be happy when he radios back from Mars to inform the advertising agency that he has completed the flight successfully, using Zerolube oil.

That was an improbable idea, and the plot unfortunately contains some pretty trite elements. Perhaps it was the successful use of character logic which overcame such disadvantages, well enough to sell it and get it reprinted across the Atlantic.

While unselfish actions tend to win sympathy for a character, the writer must guard against too much of a good thing. Black villians and snow-white heroes, set up as mere puppets of an arbitrary plot, aren't likely to ring true. Character logic is neglected. Real people just aren't that way. Very interesting conflict, I have discovered, is possible between two perfectly admirable people, who simply happen to have opposing traits. Once, in a series, I was able to use the villian of one story as the sympathetic hero of the next.

Villians, incidentally, are often easier to characterize than heroes. The fact suggests the villainous hero—the character who is made convincing by a large measure of original sin, but who is acting altruistically enough, in the story, to merit the reader's interest.

"The Crucible of Power" deals with a ruthless and unscrupulous promoter, who betrays several wives and swindles the peoples of two planets and yet finally wins the reader's forgiveness—and earns a few more millions for himself—when one of his patent medicines turns out to be a real cure.

Poor old Giles Habibula, who seems to have been the best remembered character from the "Legion of Space" trilogy, follows something of this same pattern. He is convincingly human, I think, because of his Falstaffian concern for his own comforts and safety. Yet the reader accepts him and even likes him, I believe, because at the time in question—however reluctantly and loudly complaining—he is willing to risk his own precious fat in pursuit of a cause which the reader approves.

And that, I think, outlines the best of my own laboriously acquired knowledge of fantasy-writing. I can't claim any magic for the stated rules. Many other writers in the field are able to turn out more material, doubtless with much less fuss about how they do it. For my part, I've never been able to produce much more than 100,000 words a year. Usually I find it necessary to plan a story carefully and methodically, and then write trial beginnings until the people become convincingly alive.

Any successful story, I think, even for a pulp magazine, must express some genuine feeling, and no formula will do that. Rules alone are not enough. The vital thing is to have some hot inner urge to share experience and emotion generously, to hold and move your reader, to utter something that must be said. Yet I do feel that good fantasy and science fiction must conform to the logic of premise and character, and that a proper regard for such principles might save the unwary writer from disappointing blunders.

COMPLICATION IN THE SCIENCE FICTION STORY

By A. E. van Vogt

Editor's Preface

A. E. VAN VOGT

WHEN A. E. VAN VOGT'S "Black Destroyer" appeared in *Astounding Science-Fiction* in 1939, the readers immediately acclaimed it one of the best stories of the year, and hailed its author as a new star on the S-F horizon. With the publication of "Slan" in 1940, van Vogt established himself firmly among the top writers in the field.

Alfred van Vogt was born April 26, 1912, in Winnipeg, Manitoba, Canada. He spent most of his early life in a Saskatchewan village, where his father practised law. Later, the family settled in a small Manitoba town, moving from there to Winnipeg, the capital of the province, and to a temporary affluence (when his father was general western agent of the Holland American Line). The stock market crash of 1929 brought on a return to a dependence on a law practise.

During this period van Vogt worked on a farm one season, was a separator man on a threshing outfit, drove a truck for a combine, and finally was employed for a year by the Bureau of Statistics in Ottawa, capital of Canada. This phase ended in June, 1932. In August of that year, he wrote a story which was purchased by MacFadden Publications for one of their confession magazines. During the next seven years he wrote confessions, love stories, radio plays, and a host of trade paper articles.

In 1939, two important events took place. "Black Destroyer" was published—introducing van Vogt to the field of fiction which now claims him for its own—and he married Edna Mayne Hull. It should be mentioned that Miss Hull, an author in her own right, has since gained an enviable reputation for her science fiction and fantasy.

Since 1939 van Vogt has sold approximately a million words of science fiction. Four of his stories have been included in major anthologies, and a fifth is scheduled for a forthcoming collection. Two of his novels, "Slan" and "The Weapon Makers", have been published in book form; "The Book of Ptath" will be issued by *Fantasy Press* in Autumn, 1947; and two other books, one by *Fantasy Press,* as yet unnamed, and "The World of $\overline{A}$", are scheduled for future release. It now seems fairly certain that three quarters of his million words will eventually be published in book form. In addition, van Vogt has been approached by motion picture and radio agents, though without results thus far.

In his contribution to this volume, van Vogt has offered suggestions which differ materially from those of the other writers in the series. This is not surprising, since his work is outstanding for its individuality. He has brought something new to science fiction. He may well be called "the Master of Confusion", since the multiplicity of plot threads, the wealth of ideas found in his work, particularly in his longer stories, serves to mystify the reader more thoroughly than the average "whodunit". Yet his stories end with complete clarification of every mysterious occurrence; every thread falls into its proper place in the plot fabric.

The writer who wishes to inject complication into his science fiction will find much of value in A. E. van Vogt's article. And after all, a story without *some* complication (if it can be called a story) is a drab affair indeed, with little chance of gaining a publisher's check.

COMPLICATION IN THE SCIENCE FICTION STORY

I WRITE a story with a full and conscious knowledge of technique. Whenever my mind blurs, no matter how slightly, on a point of technique, there my story starts to sag, and I have to go back, consciously think it over, spot the weakness, and repair it according to the principles by which I work.

It is these principles which I intend to describe in the following pages.

I sold my first story in 1932 (not science fiction) by rigorously adhering to one of these rules. My total wordage in science fiction, about a million words, has been produced by adherence to the same principles. And with my work beginning to appear between hard covers, and with movie and radio agents interested in my stories, the technique apparently has justified itself.

Even at this intermediate stage, it is difficult to imagine that, only twenty years ago, science fiction authors were selling their work for a third of a cent a word on publication. But then it is equally hard to believe that today atomic energy, that old standby of science fiction, is an accomplished fact. Soon, the first atomic war will also be fact and not fiction—but if you are planning to write a science fiction story leave the atomic war alone. Its fictional possibilities have been exhausted. The readers are bored by it. Your mind will have to reach out to new possibilities, not necessarily gadget ideas, but new approaches, in which the war itself is incidental. Character, mood, the wonder of it all— the character approach is far and away the best bet in the immediate future of the science fiction field.

Very well, then, let us suppose you have conceived an excellent idea for a science fiction story. Now, you are sitting down to write it. What next?

Think of it in scenes of about 800 words. This is not original with me, but I have followed that rule religiously ever since I started to write. Every scene has a purpose, which is stated near the beginning, usually by the third paragraph, and that purpose is either accomplished, or not accomplished by the end of the scene. This is so important that a few examples are justified:

> For Leigh, the first desperate shock was past. The room was curiously dim, as if he was staring out through eyes that were no longer—his!
>
> He thought with an effort at self-control: "I've got to fight. Some *thing* is trying to possess my body. All the rest is lie."

There is no doubt about the purpose in that scene from "Asylum". Does he accomplish this purpose? The scene ends:

> . . . He tried to jerk back. And couldn't. His body wouldn't move. Instantly, then, he tried to speak, to crash through the enveloping blanket of unholy silence. But no sound came.
>
> Not a muscle, not a finger stirred; not a single nerve so much as trembled.
>
> He was alone.
>
> Cut off in his little corner of brain.
>
> Lost.

Is it possible to get a scene purpose and a story purpose into the opening scene of a long story? This is one of the problems of every story, and usually it can be solved by having the story purpose grow out of the whole first scene. Still, it is interesting to get something of both the immediate and the long run purposes into the opening paragraphs. In "The Book of Ptath," a full length novel [*Fantasy Press*] laid

COMPLICATION IN THE SCIENCE FICTION STORY

in a period some two hundred million years in the future, the double statement of purpose is accomplished as follows:

> He was Ptath. Not that he thought of his name. It was simply there, a part of him, like his body and his arms and legs, like the ground over which he walked. No, that last was wrong. The ground was not of him. There was a relation, of course, a little puzzling.
>
> He, Ptath, walking on ground, walking to Ptath. Returning to the city of Ptath, capital of his empire of Gonwonlane after an absence. That much was clear, accepted without thought, and it was important. He felt the urgency of it in the way his nerves stayed tense, and in the way he kept quickening his pace to see whether the next bend of the river would make it possible for him to turn westward.

The scene purpose is for him to cross the river. Why is it important? Because he has no more idea what a river is than a road. When he finally tries to cross the river it does not occur to him to swim.

> This time he ignored the pain in his chest and walked on, straight through the liquid darkness that engulfed him. And, after a moment, as if realizing its defeat, the pain went away. . . . The twisting pain came back as he emerged finally into shallower water. . . .
>
> The paroxysm ended. He climbed to his feet and stood staring at the dark, rushing stream. He turned away finally, determined about one thing. He didn't like water.

He's across, but in crossing he has given us a picture of a god-king returning "after an absence" without the word "god" ever being used.

There is not a story of mine in which the scene pattern differs markedly from the foregoing. Naturally, every scene has its own tiny variational problems, but sooner or later, usually sooner, the purpose of the scene is plainly stated or implied so clearly that there is no doubt of what is to be accomplished.

By adopting this "secret" of the 800 word scene (it can be 600 words or a 1000 words), I wrote and sold my first story, and it has formed a solid base for all the stories I have sold since then.

Readers have a habit of being right about an author. Some years ago, in a "little" magazine—they call them fanzines in the science fiction and fantasy field—I was described as an "idea" man. Meaning that my science fiction stories abounded in ideas, twists and odd angles.

This description startled me, for I had never thought about it in that way. But, almost immediately, I recognized the accuracy of the description. Ever since I started writing for the science fiction field, it has been my habit to put every current thought into the story I happened to be working on. Frequently, an idea would seem to have no relevance, but by mulling over it a little, I would usually find an approach that would make it usable.

There are writers who warn you against putting all your ideas into one story. Hold them back, they say, for soon there will be another story coming along where they may be more useful. This has a certain logic to it, but let me issue a counter warning: The brain does not develop on negative expectations. If a person attaches too much importance to one idea, then the brain will concentrate around that idea, and will stop manufacturing new ones.

My own experience has been that the brain thrives on positivity. Take it for granted that ideas will come as you need them—and they do. Don't hoard, but start a flow. Once such a flow is under way the problem will be to turn it off, not to keep it going.

The foregoing is the general approach to the problem, rather, the necessity, of developing an abundance of new ideas. As writers quickly discover, however, every story has

COMPLICATION IN THE SCIENCE FICTION STORY

its own idea needs, special and different from the needs of all other stories. Somewhere in each new piece of fiction, the idea factory has to start manufacturing material to exact measurements.

How are these ideas developed, and where do they come from? In science fiction, the problem is both more urgent and more difficult, because the readers in this field have a sharp eye for a story that is not "original".

To begin with, an author should have an idea for the story itself. At this stage I am not a good example. My early ideas for a story are sometimes so blurred that it seems incredible that the final story developed from such a thin shadow of substance. Let us, accordingly, quickly pass to the stage where the story has taken a vague form. The main character has been named, some tentative writing has been done on odd paragraphs in an effort to establish the "feel" of the story. Or, possibly, the first version of the first scene is written. Since the scene has been written with a scene purpose, it is reasonably clearly focussed, and yet beyond is a great darkness. Where to next? What about the ending? In fact, why worry about the ending at this stage. It's practical, here, to worry about Scene Two. Or is it?

There are times when it is possible to write the end of Scene Two without knowing what is to follow. But this is rare. A story grows out of its first scene. Once you have thought about the implications of Scene One, you have at least the embryos of *several* following scenes. An example:

In the opening scene of a short story of mine, "A Can of Paint", the main character lands on Venus (the first man to land on Venus) and he finds a can of Venusian paint. It opens differently than he expects and some of it spills on him. This is annoying, but he does not regard it as serious until he discovers it won't rub off with any of the methods that he knows.

The scenes implied by the foregoing run something like this: Here is a strange paint, which seems to have some wonderful properties. What would a perfect paint be like, and how would he rub it off? One by one he discovers its properties—and entangles himself deeper and deeper, until it is on the point of killing him. One idea leads to another. Scene three, after some initial failures, begins like this:

Kilgour wrote:

"A perfect paint should be waterproof and weatherproof as well as beautiful. It should also be easily removable."

He stared gloomily at the final sentence. And then, in a fit of temper, he flung down the pencil, and walked over to the bathroom mirror. He peered into it with a nasty smirk on his face.

"Pretty, aren't you!" he snarled at his blazing image. "Like a gypsy arrayed in dance finery."

At the end of scene three, he discovered that "once applied, the ultimate paint was self renewing." As will now be seen, here idea leads to idea. Once the first scene was written, all the rest followed logically.

Another example. In a 35,000 word novelette, "The Changeling", the opening scene deals with a curious discovery by the main character. The discovery is that he doesn't know who he is. He has been going along for several years, married, living in a magnificent home, head of a big firm at an excellent salary, and then in Scene One a chance remark opens up a gulf behind him.

What does an opening like this suggest for future scenes? First, of all, it suggested to me that there must be a dividing line between his present reality and the "false" past. When did he take up his duties with the firm? By questioning his employees, he discovers that it was about four years before.

But he was married before that. Therefore, his wife knows what happened. Before confronting her, he checks on his birth certificate and on his war record. He discovers that a person of his name was born some fifty years before

COMPLICATION IN THE SCIENCE FICTION STORY

(he looks 35), and that the man lost a leg in World War II. But he has both legs.

When he finally confronts his beautiful wife with these facts, she has him locked in his room, and thereafter he is continually under guard inside the estate.

Briefly, then the sequence has been (1) Craig discovers something is wrong. (2) He checks up cautiously, afraid at first of appearing ridiculous. (3) Finally, he confronts his wife, and, though he remains in the dark about the reasons for everything, the situation is forced into the open. It required more than three scenes to write that, but it is clear that one sequence led logically to another.

The story is launched. The main character is in trouble, and his problem has been shown. His story purpose is to discover what happened. In writing this story, I knew what was behind the mystery, but the ideas of each scene grew in the way I have described.

There is one more point to bring out here. Ideas follow the 800 word scene. By this is meant that you cannot write 800 words about nothing. Having started a scene you must think of ideas to fill it out to the required length. In other words, if you find that you have solved your scene purpose at the end of 300 words, then something is wrong. The scene isn't properly developed. There are not enough ideas in it, not enough detail, not enough complication.

Never forget that 800 word scene. It's a nice thing to have around. It tells you better than abstract logic that it's time for another idea; and it had better be good, or the science fiction readers will eat you up, verbally, of course.

When the editor of this symposium suggested I write an article on complication in the science fiction story, he was saying, in effect, that that is the kind of story I write. This was as new a picture of myself as the earlier statement that I was an "idea" man. These sudden glimpses of what other people think of you come upon you like a flash; briefly you resist the identification, and then comes the partial acceptance as a thousand bits of verification drift up into your mind.

Yes, I write what might be called a complication story. I also try to introduce character, atmosphere, insight and science. But I'll come to that presently. Not so long ago, a would-be writer asked me how to write a story that was at least 5000 words long. He would get a good idea (he told me some of his ideas, and they were good), and then somehow at the end of 2000 words the story would be over, and if the rejection slip carried any comment, it was usually to the effect that the story was too long.

"Too *long!*" he cried to me, "and yet I've seen stories of yours that ran to ten thousand words, and they didn't have as much complication as mine."

I told him about the 800 word scene, and now at least he can write a long story. I forgot a couple of things, however, while I was talking to him, and since I haven't seen his name in print, I assume that he hasn't discovered these other points for himself.

A short story has to have at least two threads of "plot". The longer a story is, the more threads it has to have, but some of these can be very minor, little more than derivations of character traits. These minor threads, therefore, can be made to serve a double purpose. They sharpen the characterization, and add richness and color to the story. Minor threads can also be derived from (1) theme (2) science and (3) atmosphere. These various points will be illustrated in a moment—but first the main threads.

A short story and a novelette have a main "plot" and a secondary "plot". The secondary thread arises out of the main story and is solved with it. Theoretically, it's as simple as that. Now, let's see what it looks like in practise.

> I wakened with a start, and thought: How was Renfrew taking it?
>
> I must have moved physically, for blackness edged with pain closed over me. How long I lay in that agonized faint, I have no

COMPLICATION IN THE SCIENCE FICTION STORY

means of knowing. My next awareness was of the thrusting of the engines that drove the spaceship. Slowly this time, consciousness came. I lay very quiet, feeling the weight of my years of sleep, determined to follow the routine prescribed so long ago by Pelham. I didn't want to faint again.

I lay there, and I thought: It was silly of me to have worried about Jim Renfrew. He wasn't due to come out of his state of suspended animation for another fifty years.

The man who tells the story has just awakened after an artificial sleep lasting fifty years. He and three other men are by this method attempting to reach Alpha Centaurus, the famous nearest star system, four and a third light years from Earth. They expect it will take five hundred years, and have taken doses of the cataleptic drug to enable them to awaken one at a time at intervals of half a century.

The main story is the trip and its strange aftermath. The secondary thread is stated in the first paragraph: *"How was Renfrew taking it?"* Renfrew, owner of the ship and sponsor of the trip, is a colorful weakling. The others are worried about him, and this worry is justified for he goes insane as a result of developments in the "main" thread. It should be noted here that the secondary thread is never merely endless suspicion; if it begins as suspicion it is quickly borne out by reality. When you haven't got a good, solid, substantial secondary thread thoroughly integrated with your main thread, editors have a habit of saying, "This story is too light. It doesn't seem well rounded. The 'plot' is too thin." Many editors have never heard of the secondary thread in a story, but they do know what it feels like to read a story that hasn't got one. The story isn't complete. It has no life. It may have a good idea, but it is not fully developed.

Now, let's take a glance at the other types of minor threads, the ones that derive from theme, science and atmosphere.

In science fiction, the atmosphere story comes up again and again. The characters go to other planets. There is the beginning of atmosphere. Building it up properly requires imagination, but the story becomes richer as a result. Here is the opening of my story, "M33 in Andromeda":

> The night whispered, the immense night of space that pressed against the hurtling ship. Voiceless susurration it was, yet somehow coherent, alive, deadly. For it called, it beckoned and it warned. It trilled with a nameless happiness, then hissed with savage, unthinkable frustration. It feared and it hungered. How it hungered. It died—and reveled in its death. And died again. It whispered of inconceivable things. Wordless, all-enveloping, muttering flow. Tremendous, articulate, threatening night.

An exploring ship from Earth is heading for the nebula M33, the first time human beings have attempted to go beyond their own galaxy. Long before they reach the outer stars of the new galaxy, they run into the strange thought pressure partially described above. In this story the atmosphere develops into the main thread, with the problem of one of the human characters constituting the secondary thread. But it does illustrate how atmosphere adds richness and color and menace to a story.

A good example of the use of minor threads is my story "The Weapon Makers", a 70,000 word novel. Following is an excerpt of a review of it that appeared in the British magazine, *Fantasy Review:*

"It's a typical van Vogt set-up, which not only takes us to Alpha Centauri but introduces such minor themes as telepathy, immortality, human giantism (graced with the name of vibratory magnification), super-mentality, time travel, 'freak' planets and super-intelligent spiders. I repeat, *minor* themes . . . And formidable though it must sound to the reader for whom one such concept is enough to make a story,

COMPLICATION IN THE SCIENCE FICTION STORY

I must say that I find the peculiar hotch-potch of ultra-imaginative conception which this writer mixes so adroitly, and with such compelling interest, as convincing as it is intriguing."

What about those minor themes, for that is what they are? They added color and life to the story—but every one of them was included for a definite purpose. This novel opens up:

> A whole year had passed. The trail, Neelan thought, would be—*cold!*
>
> He sat, letting the rhythm of the superbly swift trans-State plane soothe him. It had not been his fault that he couldn't get to Earth sooner. The meteorite, where Carew and he had been doing the preliminary work on their strike of "heavy" beryllium, had just entered the Dead Spot, the extreme opposite side of the sun from Earth, when the knowledge had come that Gil was dead.

Gil is his brother. How did the knowledge come to him that Gil was dead? By a very different method than might be supposed.

> The thought . . . was like a signal to his mind. It brought memory of the sharp awareness that had come to him out there in space a year ago, his first knowledge that Gil was dead. Acute awareness it had been of the lack of that neural pressure which had constituted, even at that distance, the bond between his brother and himself. . . .
>
> . . . They had often wondered, Gil and he and the scientists, what it would be like for one to die. The scientists had taken them at the age of five, identical twins already sensitive to each other, and magnified the sensitivity until it was a warm interflow of life force, a world of dual sensation. The interrelation had grown so

sharp that at short distances (a few thousand miles) thoughts passed between them with all the clarity of the electronic flux in a local telestat.

There is the introduction to the "telepathy" theme in this story. It introduces the character as different. The old purpose of a man coming to find out what happened to his brother, always emotionally sound, but trite with overuse, has here been refurbished and remodelled.

We can skip some of the other themes, except to say that the attempt is made to introduce each one in a warmly human fashion—and pass on to what sounds like the wildest idea of all, the "super-intelligent spiders". Why, for heaven's sake, introduce such Buck Rogerish creations?

They are not in the story for the sake of added excitement. They prove the theme, which is to the effect that man shall rule the universe because of his emotional nature. They are utterly unemotional, and they themselves finally recognize that they are a doomed race for that reason. Necessary? Yes, they are. They add to the theme a strength that would otherwise be missing.

These are the kinds of threads that fill out a story, but they should never be tossed in for their own sake. They should be an integral part of a story. If you haven't got them you will find your 800 word scenes becoming very anemic.

It is well to note that the earlier discussion on how to develop ideas is very closely related to the use of complication in a story. Every new idea in a story is a complication, but there is a law to the use of ideas, which limits them slightly. The law is that a shorter length story has a main thread and a secondary thread. Everything else should further one or the other of these two important threads. It is unwise to develop a third or fourth thread to rival the first two in importance, unless you are planning a novel. Then more threads are not only desirable, they are necessary.

COMPLICATION IN THE SCIENCE FICTION STORY

I have now described in considerable detail the separate ingredients of a story. As every reader knows, however, a story is not merely an accumulation of ingredients. In science fiction, the balancing of different items, the way of bringing in science bit by bit, the building up of suspense, so that the story seems just right, must all appear to have been accomplished in a natural fashion. To the reader, a story just grows along. In my own experience this has happened only once in a while. Usually, a great deal of manipulation is necessary.

I have written stories, which, when I reached the point where I had planned to end them, were utterly hopeless. And yet, by rearranging the scenes, by writing and re-writing a few hundred words, I have managed to turn them into salable stories.

At times, a scene which I have inserted near the beginning, has proved to be the final scene of the story. It is possible to give too much information near the beginning of a story, and so ruin the excitement of the ending. There is hardly a phase of the writing of a story that is more important.

In deciding on the when, what and how of manipulating a story, I have reached the stage where I can read the story through, and just "listen" to it as I read. Hundreds of thousands of stories have been written by people who knew nothing about technique, but who did have a good "ear". Many thousands more will be written in the same way by talented people. There is one major fault with this method by itself, without any accompanying knowledge of technique. It is not consistent in its results. People who write by "ear" sell spasmodically.

This is not to say that a writer who knows his technique does not have failures, but my own development is evidence, to me at least, that a knowledge of craftsmanship is a prerequisite to consistent sales. At the beginning, when I knew very little about technique, my sales were few and far between. Now, it is the other way round.

I have found the foregoing technique more successful with the science fiction story than with any other type of story that I have ever written. I use it on every piece of fiction I turn out, consciously and deliberately.

Naturally, I shall keep on adding to it to the end of my writing career. At the moment, this is as far as I've gotten.

Good luck.

HUMOR IN SCIENCE FICTION
By L. Sprague de Camp

L. SPRAGUE DE CAMP

Editor's Preface

COMPARATIVELY little humorous science fiction and fantasy has been written; editors have never had an oversupply of this sort of material. Of the writers in the field who have specialized in humor, L. Sprague de Camp is probably the most popular — and deservedly so, since his keen sense of humor is combined with a natural flair for writing, and sound scientific training.

De Camp was born in New York City on November 27, 1907. Later the family moved to the west coast; and Sprague received his early schooling in California, graduating from Hollywood High School in 1925. He attended California Institute of Technology, graduating in 1930 with a degree of B.S. in Aeronautical Engineering. He continued his studies at Massachusetts Institute of Technology graduate school; and in 1933 received his M.S. degree in Engineering and Economics from Stevens Institute of Technology, Hoboken, N. J.

For the next few years he worked as editor, article-writer, instructor, and patent engineer. During this period he spent a year as Principal of the School of Inventing and Patenting of the International Correspondence Schools.

He began writing fiction in 1937, and became a full-time free-lance writer in 1938. Although his earlier, more conventional work was well received, de Camp did not attain his reputation as a top-flight writer until he turned his talents to humorous or semi-humorous science fiction and wacky fantasy.

During his first five years as a writer, de Camp sold approximately forty-five stories of various lengths for magazine publication, including a number of novel-length stories. He had several books published, three of them fantasy—"Lest Darkness Fall", "The Incomplete Enchanter", and "The Land of Unreason" (the latter two in collaboration with Fletcher Pratt).

In 1948 *Holt* will publish his "Round About the Cauldron: A Study of Magic, Witchcraft, and Occultism in Western Civilization"; and in the same year *Fantasy Press* plans to issue two of his short novels, "Divide and Rule" and "The Stolen Dormouse", under one cover.

World War II temporarily halted de Camp's writing career; working as a mechanical engineer for the U. S. Navy left no time for writing. He subsequently received his commission of Lieutenant in the U. S. Naval Reserve, and ended the war as Lieutenant Commander. Since the war he has returned to writing, but he continues active in the Naval Reserve.

L. Sprague de Camp's comments on the writing of humorous science fiction are particularly pertinent. He has analyzed humor, and he knows *why* humorous situations are funny. In addition, he is able to tell others how to secure humorous effects in their fiction. Finally, to give authority to his statements, he is able to do himself what he tells others to do.

Obviously, the writing of humorous fiction (science, fantasy or other) is not for everyone. The sad examples of socalled humor published during the early days of science fiction are proof that it isn't easy to be funny. But—for the writer who has inclinations in this direction, de Camp's contribution to this symposium should prove invaluable.

HUMOR IN SCIENCE FICTION

ALTHOUGH I'm supposed to be writing about the use of humor in science fiction, the fact is that there's little to be said about humor in science fiction that doesn't apply to humor generally. Certainly the rules of humor are the same in science fiction and fantasy, so don't be surprised if I seem to draw my illustrations from a wider field than that of science fiction pure.

Be that as it may, let us like good semanticists start off by deciding what we mean by humor. Humor, in the sense of this article, is simply something in a story that makes the reader smile or laugh. And what makes the reader laugh? Well, if you'll examine the jokes, gags, and funny-business that produce that desired effect on the reader, you'll find them nearly all compounded, in various proportions, of surprise, aberrancy, and inoffensiveness.

Surprise of course consists simply of leading the reader to expect one thing and giving him another. The use of surprise is shown by the well-known short short short ghost story about the man who met another man late one dark afternoon in a deserted art-gallery, and remarked that it was a spooky old place, wasn't it? "Do you believe in ghosts?" asked the second man calmly. "No, of course not," replied the first. "Do you?" "Yes," said the second man, and vanished.

The quality of aberrancy — or, if you prefer, oddity, singularity, peculiarity, or nonconformity—is more complex. Its main characteristic is incongruity—the fact that something is where, in a well-ordered world, it should never be. An opera hat is not funny at the opera, but on a cannibal chief it is out of place and therefore funny; conversely a kangaroo is not especially droll in the Australian bush, but in the Grand Central Station it at once becomes so. A man and his wife quarreling are not particularly funny ipso facto, but clothe them in the robes of royalty and they become funny, for most of us retain a hidden belief from childhood stories that kings and queens don't act that way. One of the most durable of old stage and screen comedies, "Charlie's Aunt," depends for its comic effect upon nothing more complex than the spectacle of a young bachelor posing as an elderly spinster. Thorne Smith's feat of dropping a bishop into a nudist camp, or Kaufman and Hart's notion of sending nine robed and bearded U. S. Supreme Court justices dancing athletically about a musical-comedy stage, involves such colossal incongruity that the mere idea predisposes us to laugh.

In science fiction we make great use of a particular form of incongruity—anachronism, or the misplacing of things in time. We can get a humorous effect by inserting primitive or present-day elements into a picture of a highly advanced future civilization; or (in stories of backwards time-travel) placing present-day elements in a picture of some former time; for instance, by sending a modern character back to Rome to sell Julius Caesar a derby hat.

You can even get humorous effects by fictitious anachronisms, as by having King Solomon use twentieth-century slang. It's a fictitious anachronism, because the only reason it's funny is that most readers have been conditioned by the Bible to think of Solomon as speaking the English of about 1600 A. D.—the English of the King James Bible—whereas Solomon, of course, really spoke Aramaic, and hence the English of 1947 is no greater an anachronism than that of 1600. Moreover he may, for all we know, have used Aramaic slang on occasion. Of course, any joke about a Bibical character derives added force from the incongruity of associating humor with a notably humorless document; *Proverbs* xxvii, 14: "He that blesseth his friend with a loud voice, rising early in the morning, it shall be counted a curse to him", is much funnier than it would otherwise be for just this reason.

In using another form of aberrancy—irrationalism—you cause your character to behave in a manner which the reader knows to be foolish, mistaken, or ill-advised, even though to the character his course may seem the height of good sense. In this case the reader is amused not only by the oddity of the character's behavior, but also by the fact that he can congratulate himself on his own superior wisdom. For there is a slight element of sadism in most humor; our fellow-man's calamities, provided they are not too disastrous, are funny to us. Furthermore, while irrational behavior itself can be funny on a fairly low, slapstick level, the combination of riotous irrationality of behavior with sober rationality of intent is a good deal funnier because of the added element of incongruity. Thus Thorne Smith's gang of drunken characters driving a stolen fire-engine naked around town are hilarious enough. But P. G. Wodehouse in his recent "Full Moon" gets an even more risible effect out of a character, who, though sober, is led to think that he is not only drunk but also suffering from delerium tremens. The character, a notable toper who has been warned by his doctor to lay off, starts several times to backslide, but each time he is unexpectedly confronted by another character who by well-contrived coincidence happens to be passing that way, but who the toper believes to be a figment of his d. t.'s.

The humor of irrationalism combined with good intentions and rational purpose is responsible for the perennial appeal of scenes of drunkenness, of scenes wherein a sucker is fleeced by a swindler, and of stories of mistaken identity —such as the old gag of the substitution of one identical twin for another, which Shakespeare borrowed from the Roman dramatist Plautus for his "Comedy of Errors" (via Petrarch) and which has been used hundreds of times since.

The humorist must, however, not only provide surprise and aberrancy, but also must be inoffensive in his humor.

He must avoid any of a lot of elements which will make his joke fall flat. For one thing, his character shouldn't come to any real or irreparable harm, however he may be tripped up by malignant fate and stripped of his dignity and self-possession. It's all right to pick on your character, but not to the point where the reader is sharply reminded of the many unfunny things in the universe which threaten him personally. Thus if a character fears death, but is in no real danger thereof, that's funny; but if he is really killed, or nearly so, the reader is unpleasantly reminded that the Great Night awaits him too. A lot of people who saw Chaplin's "Great Dictator" were dissatisfied because, while Chaplin's burlesque of Hitler and his satellites was funny enough, the scenes of Nazis and Jews chasing each other about in slapstick cops and robbers pursuit were entirely too reminiscent of the real and unhumorous persecution which was then taking place in Germany.

Nor should a joke, to be effective, deal with any matter about which either the joker or the reader feel too strongly. Plenty of people are willing to laugh at a joke about somebody else's religion, for instance, but bristle at any levity concerning their own. Again, the late President Roosevelt had many bitter enemies who circulated coarsely derisive jokes about him and his wife; it was interesting to watch the reactions when one of these jokes was told in a mixed crowd. The Roosevelt-haters found them unroariously funny, while the Roosevelt-admirers just looked grim or embarrassed. As another example, a friend of mine once told me scornfully that he saw nothing funny in the cartoons of the *New Yorker*. The reason, I discovered, was that the *New Yorker* was in the habit of running jokes about stupid workmen. My friend, a devout Socialist, although willing enough to see members of other economic groups held up to ridicule, was offended by jokes about workers, who to him constituted a special and sacrosanct category of mankind. Finally, a lady of my acquaintance was offended by the reel of Disney's "Fantasia" in which he burlesqued Ponchielli's "Dance of the Hours" by showing the ballet performed by

HUMOR IN SCIENCE FICTION

ostriches, hippopotami, and alligators—because the piece had been a favorite of the lady in her own ballet-dancing days.

Our ideas of humor change from time to time. Much humor is purely topical—dependent upon matters of the moment, and therefore not understood by later generations. That's why so many of the jokes in Shakespeare's comedies, which no doubt rolled 'em in the aisles originally, are to us simply incomprehensible. A writer of magazine stories, however, doesn't usually care whether later generations laugh at his jokes. The last century has seen a decline in purely verbal humor, such as puns and the giving of characters odd names, so that when in our day Evelyn Waugh tries to revive the latter form of humor by calling his characters Mr. Outrage and Mrs. Ape, his wit falls rather flat. Some humorous story-ideas, once perfectly valid, have been worked to death—such as the friendly dragon and the sociable ghost.

Again, Western culture in general has become increasingly humane—or squeamish if you prefer—during the last few centuries, so that a lot of formerly legitimate subjects for humor are no longer considered as such. Four hundred years ago humorous poets wrote comic verses about the struggles of witches and heretics as they were burned. Whereas two hundred years ago cripples were deemed funny, we now say "as funny as a crutch" to denote complete humorlessness. A century ago insanity was a subject of hilarity; fifty years ago racial and religious minorities were still fair game for the jokester. Nowadays such jokes are regarded as at best in doubtful taste; some of them can still be circulated privately but cannot be published. Formerly the victim of such a joke was not thought of as human at all, but as a sort of inanimate prop to be exploited by the jester with impunity; now the reader knows too much about the tragic side of death, or of being a handicapped person, or a Negro, and so on, and doesn't care to be reminded of it as part of a joke.

On the other hand, while these tabus have been rising, others have been lowered, so that today you can joke much more freely about the once sacred institutions of the government, the clergy, and sex than was formerly the case. (You can't make fun of God, however, who still has many admirers.)

You've all heard of the Polynesian word *tabu*, meaning "sacred, fearsome, untouchable", but perhaps you don't know that it has an antonym *noa,* meaning "profane, vulgar, commonplace". Now, when a thing is altogether tabu you can't joke about it for fear of punishment—even if the punishment is only the disapproval of your friends. If the thing is *noa* there's no point in joking about it because it's too commonplace to provide the incongruity and surprise of humor. But when a thing is in between—say, something whose former strict tabu is now breaking down—it becomes a good subject for humor based upon the contrast between the solemnity with which a tabued subject is supposed to be treated and the levity of the jokester. For instance, we live in an age when the ancient and strict nudity-tabu of Western culture is breaking down, and therefore nudity is an excellent subject for humor; it still makes us feel a little naughty to joke about it, and at the same time we know that nothing will happen to us because we do. Hence Thorne Smith's "The Bishop's Jaegers" is one long nudity-gag, and Schuyler Miller, A. M. Phillips, and other science-fiction writers have all used it at one time or another; I exploited it in several of my own stories. However, if we Westerners ever become as casual about nakedness as the ancient Greeks, nudity will be *noa* and no longer funny.

Humor should be distinguished from burlesque and satire. Burlesque is extreme exaggeration or grotesque incongruity, and satire is an attempt to discredit some existing institution or condition, usually by means of mild burlesque. (People have sometimes accused me of writing satire, but actually I've written very little of it, unless you consider "The Stolen Dormouse" a mildly satirical spoofing of certain aspects of capitalism.) Satire may be funny, but to be successful it requires two conditions, both in rather short supply at present: a stable social order with well-established conventions, some or all of which the satirist wishes to deride; and an attitude of fundamental friendliness toward or sympathy with at least some of the people you're dealing with.

Now, we certainly don't have a stable social order at present, living as we do in an era when all the fountains of the great deep are broken up. And while some would-be satirists are sympathetic toward some group such as the working class or the Chinese or somebody, their violent antipathies and indignations make them incapable of writing good humorous satire, however effective they may be at polemics and jeremiads. Violent anger and hatred are simply incompatible with humor, since seriousness is after all the opposite of humor, and you can't expect to be both very serious and very funny about any subject at the same time. One of the most dismal attempts at humor I ever saw was a book of Communist cartoons, "The Ruling Clawss;" the trouble was not that the cartoonists weren't good at their trade, but that they were filled with such a frenzy of hatred against the bourgeoisie and the capitalists that the result was about as funny as the jokes in an 1880 issue of *Punch*.

In fact, you might even say that the celebrated social consciousness so highly praised nowadays is hostile to humor, for it presupposes a tendency to take things seriously. Perhaps the wide cultivation of social consciousness today accounts for the fact that so little good humorous fiction is written at present. Instead, we get interminable social-significance stories about the tedious lives of stupid people living in a dull place where nothing ever happens.

So, while a social consciousness is no doubt a fine thing to have, you'd better park yours on the shelf any time you want to be funny, just as you park your scientific skepticism when you read or write a fantasy. Not only does the intrusion of serious matter into humor spoil the humor, but the humor is apt to weaken the serious matter too; they just don't mix. When a first-rate comedian like Chaplin or the late Will Rogers gets the idea that he'd like to be a philosopher, despite a lack of the mental equipment and educational background necessary for competent philosophizing, the result is likely to be depressing.

The mere fact that a narrative depends for its appeal upon humor doesn't excuse the author from writing a good story. The yarn still needs structure, characterization, movement, narrative hook, build-up, climax, and all the rest. MacCormac succeeded so magnificently with his "Enchanted Week End" because his tale had all the qualities of a good story as well as its humor; it had a well-thought-out structure and followed logically from its assumptions. It's an easy and fatal mistake to think that because you've discovered some good gag, such as an amusing dialect or a bizarre personality, you can dispense with anything else. For example in my Johnny Black stories I started with a good enough concept—my intelligent bear—but in trying to make four stories out of that concept I had to strain harder and harder with each successive story to try to keep it up to the standard of those that had gone before.

So, you see, humor, whether in science fiction or elsewhere, depends upon surprise, aberrancy, and inoffensiveness. Science fiction stories often use the humor of anachronism, and take advantage of the present breakdown of certain tabus in our culture, such as the nudity-tabu, but otherwise they follow the same general rules as other humorous stories. While humor can help any story, a humorous story, strictly speaking, must still have all the qualities of a good story, but on the other hand mustn't allow the intrusion of much serious matter, or things about which either the writer or the reader have strong emotional feelings.

If you follow these rules you *may* be able to write a humorous science fiction story, though I wouldn't for a minute guarantee it. On the other hand if you transgress them you'll make very serious difficulties for yourself. While you may think you have good reasons for such transgressions, you probably won't amuse your readers—which is, after all, the main reason for writing a humorous story in the first place.

THE EPIC OF SPACE
By Edward E. Smith, Ph.D.

Editor's Preface

EDWARD E. SMITH, Ph.D.

ALMOST twenty years ago the name Edward Elmer Smith, Ph.D., first appeared in the pages of a science fiction magazine. His first story, "The Skylark of Space", a book-length space epic written in collaboration with Lee Hawkins Garby, struck the readers of the period with a tremendous impact, for it introduced a brand new type of science fiction writing. With the subsequent publication of the "Skylark's" two sequels and "Spacehounds of IPC" (recently reissued by *Fantasy Press* in book form), Smith laid the groundwork for the "super-physics" field of science fiction. "The Skylark of Space", by the way, was one of the first stories to use atomic energy as a major factor in its development.

Edward E. Smith was born in Sheboygan, Wisconsin, on May 2, 1890. His boyhood was spent in Spokane, Washington, and on a 160-acre homestead in Idaho. Studying at home, Smith acquired enough knowledge to pass the eighth-grade examinations and enrolled in the Prep School of the University of Idaho in 1907. He was a student during most of the next seven years. Money being scarce, however, he became at various times a mill-hand, a railroader, a miner, a street-car conductor, a teamster, a carpenter, an electrician, an asphalt-crew foreman, a stevedore, a shipping clerk, and finally a surveyor.

Graduating in 1914 as a Chemical Engineer, Smith secured a position as a food chemist in the Bureau of Chemistry, Washington, D. C. Liking the work, and being very short on fundamental organic chemistry, he went back to school. In 1915 he married Jeannie Craig MacDougall, of Boise, Idaho; she worked as a stenographer to help him get his M.S. and Ph.D. degrees.

Smith writes as a hobby, and he writes primarily to please himself. He is a slow, careful worker, which is one reason for the excellence of his work. Most of his stories are novel length (100,000 words), revealing a tremendous breadth of imagination, and an ability to handle breath-taking concepts that is truly extraordinary.

Of all the writers who produce novel length stories of interplanetary or interstellar space, Smith is best qualified to write about their construction. Himself a pioneer in the field, he has grown with it. Today his fan followers are legion. And even among his fellow science fiction writers there are many who acknowledge their indebtedness for inspiration and ideas to Edward E. Smith.

The writing of an epic of space obviously is not a small undertaking. Indeed, it is probably the most ambitious project the science fiction writer may attempt — which is our reason for placing Smith's article near the end of the series. However, it should be pointed out that, though the novel length interplanetary story may lie beyond a writer's abilities or desires, much of what Smith suggests will apply with equal force to shorter stories.

Dr. Smith's article warrants your careful consideration and analysis. There's a lot of advice in it which on the surface may not appear to be advice at all—the matter of his studying the work of other writers in the field, for example. He outlines his method of working, and in so doing offers a plan which you way well be able to follow. His last comment is highly important: if you want to write, write!

THE EPIC OF SPACE

HOW do I write a space story? The question is simple and straightforward enough. The answer, however, is not; since it involves many factors.

What do I, as a reader, like to read? Campbell, de Camp, Heinlein, Leinster, Lovecraft, Merritt, Moore, Starzl, Taine, van Vogt, Weinbaum, Williamson—all of these rate high in my book. Each has written more than one tremendous story. They cover the field of fantastic fiction, from pure weird to pure science fiction. While very different, each from all the others, they have many things in common, two of which are of interest here. First, they all put themselves into their work. John Kenton *is* Abraham Merritt; Jirel of Joiry *is* Catherine Moore. Second, each writes—or wrote—between the lines, so that one reading is not enough to discover what is really there. Two are necessary—three and four are often-times highly rewarding. Indeed, there are certain stories which I still re-read, every year or so, with undiminished pleasure.

Consider Merritt, for instance. He wrote four stories—"The Ship of Ishtar", "The Moon Pool", "The Snake Mother", and "Dwellers in the Mirage"—which will be immortal. A ten-year-old child can read them and thrill at the exciting adventurous surface stories. A poet can read them over and over for their feeling and imagery. A philologist can study them for their perfection of wording and phraseology. And yet, underlying each of them, there is a bed-rock foundation of philosophy, the magnificence of which simply cannot be absorbed at one sitting.

OF WORLDS BEYOND

In this connection, how many of you have read, word by word, the ascent to the Bower of Bel, in "The Ship of Ishtar"? Those who have not, have missed one of the most sublime passages in literature. And yet a friend of mine told me that he had skipped "that stuff". It was too dry!

These differences in reader attitude, however, bring up the very important matter of treatment. It is a well-known fact that many readers, particularly those whose heads are of use only in keeping their ears apart, want action, and only action. Slambang action; the slammier and the bangier the better. It is also a fact that some editors will either reject or rewrite stories which do not conform to such standards. Since it is practically impossible to read such a story twice, however, the type is mentioned only in passing.

Something besides action, then, is necessary. What? And how much? And should the characters grow, or not? Many writers—good ones, at that—do not let their characters grow. It is easier. Also, it allows a series of stories about the same characters to go on practically endlessly; being limited only by the readers' patience. Personally, I like to have my characters grow and develop; even though this growth limits sharply the number of stories I am able to write about them.

It would seem as though anyone, after a few days or weeks of study of any good book on "How to Write the Great American Novel", could emerge with a clear understanding of such basic things as plot, conflict, situation, incident, suspense, interest, treatment, and atmosphere; but, unfortunately, I didn't. Authorities differ. I don't know yet whether there are three basic plots, or eleven, or whether an author has a brand-new plot when he changes his hero from a bright young lawyer to a brilliant young physicist, and his heroine from a wise-cracking brunette stenographer to a witty blonde stewardess. I don't know yet whether the incomparable Weinbaum's "Trweel", which — or who? — rocked Fandom on its foundations, was a new plot, a new school of thought, or an incident. So, while I will probably

THE EPIC OF SPACE

use some of those words, I will use them in the ordinary, and not in the technical, sense.

Besides action, a good story must have background material and atmosphere to give authority, authenticity, and verisimilitude. It must also have characterization—character-drawing—to make its people real people and not marionettes dancing at the end of the author's string. To balance these factors is not easy, since they are mutually almost exclusive—not entirely so, since much can be shown in action sequences—and since the slower-moving material must not detract too much from that intangible, indefinable asset which writers and editors call "story value".

Nor does the choice lie entirely, or even mostly, with the author; for the public cannot read stories which editors will not publish. I wrote three stories (not scientific fiction) which were not slanted, but which were written exactly as I wanted to write them. I liked them; but editors did not. Hence they will remain unpublished.

Character-drawing, however deftly or interestingly it is done, does operate to slow down the action of a story. Background material and atmosphere are usually slower still. Philosophy, even in small doses, is slowest of all. Yet any story, if it is to live beyond the month of its publication, must be balanced. Hence the often-heard accusation of "wordiness" hurled at so many writers is almost never justified. I do not believe that any author writes words merely to fill up space. He uses words just as a mechanic uses tools or as an artist uses colors and brushes, and with just as definite an aim in view. The casual reader may not know, or care, what that end is, but in practically every case the author has known exactly what he was trying to do with every one of those words. He may have been using them for atmosphere, for character-drawing, for a subtle imagery or philosophy perceptible only to the reader able and willing to read between the lines, or for any one of a dozen other purposes. Thus, the action fan begrudges every word which does not hurl the story along; and does not like Lovecraft, saying that he is "wordy". To the reader who likes and appreciates atmosphere, however, Lovecraft was the master craftsman.

Some authors are better than others, of course. There are poor mechanics, too; and poor artists. For that matter, I wonder if any artist ever painted a picture that was as good as he wanted and intended it to be?

Great stories must be logical and soundly motivated; and it is in these respects that most "space-operas"—as well as more conventional stories—fail. A story must have action, conflict, and suspense. An author must get his hero into a jam; and, whether or not he really *must* marry him off, he usually does so, either actually or by implication. Now it is (or at least it should be) apparent that if the hero has even half of the brain with which the author has so carefully endowed him, he is not going to land his spaceship and, without examination or precaution, gallop heedlessly away from it, specifically to be captured by ferocious natives. Yet how often that precise episode has occurred, for exactly that reason! Similarly, if anyone connected with the take-off of a rocket-ship — especially an experimental model—had any fraction of a brain, there would be just about as much chance of a beautiful female stowing away aboard it as there would be in the case of a 500-mile racer at Indianapolis. Yet that atrocity has been used sickeningly often, to introduce effortlessly an interference with the hero's plans and to drag in by the heels a love interest that does not belong there.

Now sound, solid motivation is far from easy—a fact which accounts for the rather widespread use of coincidence. This dodge, while not as bad as some other crimes, reveals mental laziness—excepting, of course, when it is an element in mass-production methods of operation.

I have found motivation the hardest part of writing; and several good men have told me that I am not alone. It takes work—*plenty* of work—to arrange things so that even a really smart man will be forced by circumstances to get into situations that make stories possible. It takes time and

THE EPIC OF SPACE

thought; and many times it requires extra words and background material whose purpose is not immediately apparent.

To refer to an example with which I am thoroughly familiar, what possible motive force would make Kimball Kinnison, an adult, brilliant, and highly valued officer of the Galactic Patrol, go willingly into a hyper-spatial tube which bore all the ear-marks of a trap set specifically for him? I could not throw this particular episode into the circular file, as I have done with so many easier ones, because it is the basis of the grand climax of the final Lensman story, "Children of the Lens". Nor could I duck the issue or slide around it, since any weakness at that point would have made waste paper of the whole book. Kinnison *had* to go in. His going in had to be inevitable, with an inevitability apparent to his wife, his children, and—I hope and believe—even to the casual reader. That problem had me stumped for longer than I care to admit; and its solution necessitated the introduction of seemingly unimportant background material into "Galactic Patrol", which was published in 1937, and into the two other Lensman novels which have appeared since.

Now to go into the way in which I write a space story—specifically, the "Lensman" series, since it is in reality one story. Early in 1927, shortly after the "Skylark of Space" was accepted by the old *Amazing,* I began to think seriously of writing a space-police novel. It had to be galactic, and eventually inter-galactic, in scope; which would necessitate velocities vastly greater than that of light. How could I do it? The mechanism of the "Skylark", even though employing atomic energy, would not do. There simply wasn't enough of it, as several mathematicians pointed out to me later in personal correspondence—and as both Dr. Garby and I knew at the time. Also, the acceleration employed would have flattened out steel springs, to say nothing of human bodies, into practically monomolecular layers. Mrs. Garby and I knew that, too—but since the "Skylark" was psuedo-science, and since it was written long before the advent of scientific fiction, we could and did use those two mathematically indefensible mechanisms. This space-police yarn, however, would have to be scientific fiction.

I would not use mathematically impossible mechanics, such as that too-often-revived monstrosity of a second satellite hiding eternally from Earth behind the moon. Since the inertia of matter made it impossible for even atomic energy to accelerate a space-ship to the velocity I had to have, I would have to do away with inertia. Was there any mathematical or philosophical possibility, however slight, that matter could exist without inertia? There was—I finally found it in no less an authority than Bigelow (Theoretical Chemistry—Fundamentals). Einstein's Theory of course denies that matter can attain such velocities, but that did not bother me at all. It is still a theory—velocities greater than that of light are not *absolutely* mathematically impossible. That is enough for me. In fact, the more highly improbable a concept is—short of being contrary to mathematics whose fundamental operations involve no neglect of infinitesimals—the better I like it.

Other great drawbacks, philosophical or logical rather than mathematical, were the difficulties of communicating with strange races and the apparent impossibility of having my policemen invent or develop an identifying symbol which all good citizens would recognize but which malefactors could not counterfeit. The only emblems which I could devise led, one and all, to the old "deus ex machina" plot, which therefore was the one I adopted; with, of course, details tailored to fit the broad scheme I had in mind and to put in a new twist or two.

Having the Lensmen's universe fairly well set up, I went through my collection, studying and analyzing every "cops-and-robbers" story on my shelves: from Canstantinescu's "War of the Universes", which I did not consider a masterpiece, up to the stories of Starzl and Williamson, who wrote literature worthy of the masters they are. I then wrote to the editor of *Astounding,* describing my idea briefly and asking whether or not he considered it advisable to go ahead with it, in view of the good work already done in the field.

He wrote back one of the most cheering letters I have ever received. I will not quote it exactly, but its gist was that it was not the pioneers in any field who did the best work, but some fellow who, coming along later, could take advantage of their strengths and avoid their weaknesses—and he thought that I could deliver the goods.

Thus encouraged to go ahead (I always did do better work while being patted on the back than while being kicked in the seat of the pants) I drew up the preliminary, very broad outline. As fundamentals, I had inertialessness and the Lens. I had the Arisians and their ultimate opponents, the Eddorians. I had a sound psychological reason why the real nature of the fundamental conflict should never be made known to any member of Homo Sapiens; since that knowledge would have set up an ineradicable inferiority complex throughout the Patrol.

It soon became evident that the story could not be told in a hundred thousand words. There would have to be at least three stories; and when the outline was done, it called for four. The point then arose: how could each book be ended without leaving loose ends dangling all over the place? I have never liked unfinished novels—I fairly gritted my teeth when Edgar Rice Burroughs left Dejah Thoris locked up in a doorless cell while he wrote the next book!

By taking the Boskonians one echelon at a time, the first two yarns could be ended satisfactorily enough. The third, however, was getting so close to the ultimate conflict that I had to do one of two things, neither of which I liked: either leave loose ends or apparently use the ancient and whiskery device of the "mad scientist". After some experimental writing, I adopted the latter course. Please note, however, that neither I as the author nor Mentor of Arisia ever said anywhere that Fossten was either mad or an Arisian; although I have had, time and again, to go over the whole episode word by word to convince certain critics of the truth of this statement.

From the first quarter of the broad, general outline, only a few pages long, I made a more detailed outline of "Galactic Patrol"; laying out at the same time a graph of the structure, the progression of events, the alterations of characters, the peaks of emotional intensity and the valleys of characterization and background material. Each peak was a bit higher than the one before, as was each valley floor, until the climax was reached; after which the graph descended abruptly. My graphs are beautiful things. Unfortunately, however, while I can't seem to work without something of the kind, I have never yet been able to follow one at all closely. My characters get away from me and do exactly as they damn please, which accounts for my laborious method of writing.

I write the first draft with a soft pencil, upon whatever kind of scratch-paper is handiest. This draft is a mess; so full of erasures, interlineations, marginal notes, and cross-overs to the other side of the paper that I can't read it myself after it gets cold. The second draft is written, a day or so later, from the first—with variations. It is also in pencil, but isn't so messy; except when radical changes are necessitated by departures from the outline a few chapters later. My wife can read most of it, and she types what we call the "typescript"; in reality the third rough draft. This draft, in various stages of completion, is read and heatedly discussed by the Galactic Roamers; a fan club in Michigan—and Los Angeles. Comments and suggestions are written on the margins; on some hotly-contested points they cover the entire backs of pages. I accept and use the ideas which I think are better than my own original ones; I reject the others. By rights, these friends of mine should have their names on the title-pages and a share of the loot, but to date I have been able to resist the compulsion to give them their dues.

From the typescript, after the last "final" revision, my wife types the "original", which goes to Campbell. And as soon as it has been shipped I always wish that I had it back, to spend a few more weeks on the rough spots.

THE EPIC OF SPACE

I have already mentioned the Galactic Roamers as a group. E. E. Evans pointed out the fact that "Triplanetary", having been laid in the Lensman universe, should be, was, and MUST BE the first story of the Lensman series, instead of "Galactic Patrol". Ed Counts found flaws and suggested corrections in my handling of the Red Lensman in the grand climax. The planet Trenco was designed and computed, practically in toto, by an aeronautical engineer who was in part responsible for the *Lightning,* the *Constellation,* and the *Shooting Star.* Dr. James Enright, of Hawaii, psychologist and psychiatrist, solved some of my knottiest problems. Dr. Richard W. Dodson, neuclear physicist, helped a lot. So did Heinlein. So did many others, not only in the United States, but also in such widely-separated places as Australia, Sweden, China, South Africa, Egypt, and the Philippines. It is bromidic, but true, to say that two heads are better than one. It has been my experience that fifty are still better.

In conclusion, if you want to write a space epic, go to it. This is the way I do it. The remuneration per hour does not compare with what a bricklayer earns, and it's harder work—I have done them both, and know. However, I get a terrific kick out of writing; especially out of the fact that quite a good many people really like my stuff.

Besides, you may find a way that is easier or better than mine: maybe one that is both easier and better.

THE SCIENCE OF SCIENCE FICTION WRITING
By John W. Campbell, Jr.

JOHN W. CAMPBELL, JR.

Editor's Preface

JOHN W. CAMPBELL, JR., editor, author and nuclear physicist, made his entry into the world on June 8, 1910, at Newark, N. J. John W., Senior, was an engineer with the American Telephone and Telegraph Co., and quite early in life young John began following in his father's footsteps. Youthful experiments with outlandish contrivances have continued in recent years as more or less serious scientific research.

Following a conventional grammar and high school career, Campbell attended Duke University and Massachusetts Institute of Technology, finishing in 1933. He specialized in nuclear physics while at college because he had become deeply interested in the atomic field through reading science fiction in the old *Amazing Stories* and other publications. These, and his college courses, inspired him to try his own hand at science fiction writing. His work sold from the very beginning, his first story, "When the Atoms Failed", appearing in 1930.

For the next seven years Campbell contributed a large volume of excellent science fiction to the leading publications in the field, both under his own name and as Don A. Stuart. Then, in 1937 Street & Smith Publications persuaded him to take on the vacated editorship of *Astounding Stories* (now *Astounding Science Fiction*), a position he has held ever since. His fiction continued to appear until 1939, when, with the editing of *Unknown* in addition to *Astounding Science Fiction*, he no longer had time for writing. Campbell claims he now gets other writers to do all the work, instead of having to do it himself.

In addition to doing editorial work for the National Defense Research Council during the war, and being made Science Editor for Street & Smith, Campbell more recently became editor of *Air Trails and Science Frontier*. Despite this added work, he somehow found time to write a book, "The Atomic Story", which *Holt* published early in 1947. Some of his titles are being discussed for possible publication in book form under the *Fantasy Press* imprint.

Campbell's personal hobbies include photography, electronics, and amateur radio. Despite his varied activities, he has also managed to acquire a wife and two children. The latter two, quite appropriately, are believed by the neighbors to operate on atomic energy.

In his contribution to this symposium, John W. Campbell, Jr., speaks as both writer and editor. As a writer, he was one of the pioneers in the field, helping to shape future science fiction during the formative years. His science fiction, while he wrote, was consistently good; and much of it, even today, ranks with the very best in the field.

As an editor, Campbell has played a greater part in the development of modern, mature science fiction than any other individual. By introducing the work of men like Heinlein, van Vogt and de Camp—by helping writers develop their stories—by giving them story ideas—in these and in other ways his influence has made itself felt.

His article is a suitable climax for the series, emphasizing points previously mentioned, stressing others which were overlooked. And what more appropriate place could be found than the end of a book for an editor's comments—the editor always has the last word!

THE SCIENCE OF SCIENCE FICTION WRITING

THE author's effort in science fiction writing, or any other type of writing, is to please the editor sufficiently to make a sale. The editor's job is somewhat different—and a lot more amorphous—he's got to please a vague, uncertain, and largely inarticulate something called "the readers". The editor is an individual who can be seen and consulted by authors; the reader's only articulate expression, really, is a silent vote of No Purchase.

The editor, therefore, has to feel his way along by personal reactions, personal opinions, and consultation with his soul and the circulation manager. Eventually he develops something that might be termed a "formula" or a "philosophy" depending on your view of things. Let's call it a philosophy—for a philosophy is inherently a personal thing, and editing is necessarily a personal business. What follows, then, is simply what I believe is needed in a good science fiction story.

To be science fiction, not fantasy, an honest effort at prophetic extrapolation of the known must be made. Ghosts can enter science fiction—if they're logically explained, but not if they are simply the ghosts of fantasy. Prophetic extrapolation can derive from a number of different sources, and apply in a number of fields. Sociology, psychology and parapsychology are, today, not true sciences; therefore instead of forecasting future results of applications of sociological science of today, we must forecast the *development of a science* of sociology. From there the story can take off.

On the other hand, physics is, today, a real science, and predictions must be based on the known data of the existing science. The difference is real; we *know* what radio waves of the 20 to 40 megacycle band will do, what the properties of carbon 14 are. No science fiction story can legitimately state that these waves, or that isotope, have properties other than the known properties. But science fiction stories are much freer in the less firmly established fields of the still unfinished sciences. And because we are human beings, the human sciences are, actually, more interesting to contemplate.

For, above all else, a story—science fiction or otherwise—is a story of human beings. Even if a dog is the central character, we're actually projecting human qualities into that central character, and watching only the human-like characteristics of the dog, not his four feet and bushy tail. It it's a thinking robot that's the hero, then the robot is either made practically human, or is aligned against human characters for whom we're rooting.

In older science fiction, the Machine and the Great Idea predominated. Modern readers—and hence editors!—don't want that; they want stories of people living in a world where a Great Idea, or a series of them, and a Machine, or machines, form the background. But it is the man, not the idea or machine that is the essence.

Actually, in science fiction, ideas are peculiarly tricky things. They come in three sizes; good, bad, and indifferent. Story handling technique, and ability to write come in the three same sizes, too. And the results of a mesalliance of the three qualities can be most 'orrid. A really red-hot, superpowered, exceptionally good idea, moderately well written in a moderately well handled story will almost certainly add up to a disappointing and even annoying story. An indifferent grade idea, on the other hand, equally moderate in technique of handling and writing can turn out to be a very satisfactory piece. While a worn-out old idea with holes in its soles and over-run heels, handled by an expert can make a very good, and even a very powerful yarn.

THE SCIENCE OF SCIENCE FICTION WRITING

If you doubt that last statement, consider two stories: L. Sprague de Camp's "The Exhalted", and Jack Williamson's recent "With Folded Hands . . . ". In "The Exhalted", de Camp took what is perhaps the oldest of all science-fiction ideas, the most over-worked, hackneyed plot of 'em all—the mad genius plot—and went to town with it. Because his technique was to take the idea literally; his scientist was mad, so, properly, he was locked in the padded cell department. But he was a mad *genius,* so they couldn't keep him locked up. He could think his way out faster than they could put him in.

Williamson's yarn took what is probably the second-oldest idea in science-fiction—the robot, and his helpful services—and by proper handling made it a genuinely powerful yarn. Did it make you angry and frustrated when you finished it? A very hackneyed idea it is, that of the robot that obeys and serves and protects mankind. But Williamson, using almost precisely the basic technique Camp used in his story, looked at the idea literally, very closely, and very carefully described exactly what it meant. De Camp's story was, both technically and in practice, a comedy; Williamson's was a tragedy.

The old advice that, if you want to write, you should study the experts, doesn't mean that you should merely read their stories, but that you should see why they did the story that way—what they did that made the difference between another yarn and a bell-ringer. The basic trick on that I'll come back to; each of those two stories—and scores more that I could name such as MacDonald's "By His Bootstraps" based on the corney old hackneyed time-travel idea—have used, and used powerfully, the old, weak, worn-out ideas and made powerful reading.

You don't see many stories with powerful ideas and weak handling—I see them, weep bitter tears, and return them. The story with a powerful idea and a moderately good handling is disappointing, dissatisfying. The author had such a lovely concept—and made so little use of it that he's just spoiled a wonderful story for someone who could handle it *right*. Or he's given a fine, honest idea a very dirty deal. More than one author has gotten a rejection from *Astounding Science Fiction* with the explanation that his idea is so strong that the only moderately good handling makes for annoyance in the reader. Some of the regular authors fall victim to just such a trap. One of our good, regular authors turned in a story a while back that had a rather minor sort of incident, handled in a moderately good way—but the incident involved a very powerful theme, capable of, and worthy of, a full, careful development. The story was returned, with comments. The third rewrite, and that meant replotting, completely, with complete change of viewpoint and locale, not a simple rewording, was accepted—and was a strong yarn all the way through.

Don't try to sell "idea stories"; you may be offered something for the idea, so it can be turned over to a competent writer. Instead, take two months off and think over the ramifications of the idea, mentally trying half a dozen ways of applying it, and do the job right. People read magazines; ideas don't carry two-bit pieces around with 'em. And if you want to interest people, you have to tell stories about people, and the reactions of people.

An idea is important only in how it reacts on people, and in how people react to it. Whether the idea is social, political, or mechanical, we want people involved in and by it. And in doing that, it's worth remembering why, in essence, a reader hires an author—which is, in essence, what he is doing when he buys a magazine.

The reader wants the author to do one of two basic things—and prefers the author who does both. The author's function is to imagine for the reader, of course—but he must either (a) imagine in greater detail than the reader has, or (b) imagine something the reader hasn't thought of. Ideally, the author imagines something new, in greater detail.

Williamson's "With Folded Hands . . ." is a perfect example of imagining in greater detail. The basic idea of

THE SCIENCE OF SCIENCE FICTION WRITING

building the robots that will stop man's wars, do man's work, and rebuild man's ruined world was simple, obvious, and seemed fine. Only when the fine details of the idea were developed did the attached penalty show up—and by going after those fine details, Williamson developed a powerful story.

Isaac Asimov's robot story series is a similar detailed consideration of the application of his relatively simple "three laws of robotics".

Anson MacDonald's "Solution Unsatisfactory" was a major yarn when it appeared—and has grown in stature steadily since the atomic bomb fell. It was simply a *detailed* consideration of how men and nations would react to the presence of a weapon for which there was no defense.

The idea that it takes something "great and noble and new" in the way of an idea to make a good science-fiction story is basically wrong; it takes a new and detailed viewpoint, a real consideration of an idea or concept, to make the really powerful stories. Only with the backing of such patient *and detailed* analysis can the author earn his keep—do for the reader what the reader is actually seeking.

The author tries to please the editor, and the editor tries to figure out what the reader wants—so the basic problem is to please the reader, to give him what he wants (even though the reader himself doesn't realize what that is) in the way he wants it. Writing is, necessarily, a form of applied psychology, and good writing involves factors no grammarian ever seems to take into account. The writer must be a combination of jack-leg psychologist, grammarian, dramatist, and dreamer, and the first of these is the greatest thereof.

Consider the fate of the first person story. There are some that are great, some are good, but I am in a position to assure you that 99% of them are *not* good. And in any case, the man who attempts a first-person story is asking for trouble, and starting off with a handicap. The reason is relatively simple, but also easy to overlook. The "I" story has a strong tendency to be introspective; you get into the man's mind, hear what he's thinking. Now if we were a race of telepaths, that would be normal—but we aren't, and it isn't. I've never listened in on any one else's thoughts; to do so gives a vague sense of unease. Using the single viewpoint implied in the first person story adds another handicap to the unease of the hear-me-think factor. For special uses, it can be that a story requires the first-person presentation. But third-person is better at least 90% of the time.

In third person, the author describes what the character did, how he looked when he did it, and the tone of voice he used when he spoke. Those are things we observe daily; those are the clues we normally use in guessing at how a man is feeling, what he's thinking, and the like. Because we are accustomed to them, they are far more realistic to us than any first-person description of thoughts.

Further helping the third-person handling is the fact that people differ so widely in their mental processes. A system of thought normal to *A* may seem stiff and unnatural to *B*, and loose and unrealistic to *C*. But *A, B,* and *C* will agree that a man who walks jerkily around the room while talking and waving his hands in strong gestures, a man who puts a freshly lit cigarette down in an ash tray, takes one argumentative turn around the room, and lights another cigarette as he does—is almost hysterically keyed-up. The third-person description gives any person a thorough insight into that character's mental state. No amount of first-person, "At that time, I was violently keyed-up, pacing the floor in almost hysterical tension . . ." could be as convincing. For one thing, the Anglo-Saxon cultural pattern has indoctrinated us with the proposition that a man should never discuss in public his emotional reactions, except with the most powerful understatement. On the order of, "Watching the atomic bomb dropping toward me made me nervous".

This same general thesis—that people will agree on how a frightened man looks, but won't agree on what constitutes an adequate horror to frighten him—is particularly applicable in spine-chillers, either fantasy or science-fiction. It applies in love stories or horror stories, because each is an effort to transmit an impression of emotion. The trick is to describe the horrified, not the horror, describe the love-struck, not the lady-love. Some like blondes, some like brunettes, and won't agree on what constitutes perfect beauty. But practically anybody will agree on a general symptomology of acute love. Some don't mind green snakes with purple wings and venom-dripping fangs, while some do. But they'll both agree that a man with staring eyes and gurgling mumble, backing off half-crouched with his hands clawed, outstretched before his face, has seen something that he thought was thoroughly horrible. That trick was used fully in "Who Goes There?" by Don A. Stuart. The monster in the piece is never described beyond the very vague suggestion of "three red eyes and hair like blue earthworms". But detailed descriptions of the revulsion it arouses in the men who see it is supplied. Since the eye-witnesses report it is a particularly nasty monster—the reader doesn't demand descriptive proof that it is horrid. In first-person telling, description would be practically demanded.

Those are some of the basic considerations of technique of handling the material. The more general ones—if it's a short story, it has to be something more than description of an idea, and if it's longer than a short story, it must be more than an incident, for instance—are points that tend to be obvious to any man who has that inherent gift of stringin' a yarn that the true author has to have. And all short story courses, books like this one on how to write, and coaching notwithstanding, my experience is that authors are born, not made. Many of *Astounding Science Fiction's* best authors have sold us the first story they submitted. Heinlein, van Vogt and de Camp, for instance. Asimov didn't sell the first dozen he submitted; his work improved steadily thereafter, too. But he did have the understanding of what makes a yarn from the first. If you lack that subtle critical understanding, it can't, apparently, be taught.

Much the same applies to "style"—a thing that is six stages more tenuous and about one tenth as definable as a ghost, and yet makes the difference between a "nice idea, too bad he can't write" story and a bell-ringing, smash-hit yarn. And it's like finger-prints; every author's style is different.

Essentially, it is based on the way an author puts his ideas into English. The words he uses, and the way he uses them. Some authors excell at a flow of wording so smooth, with so much rhythm in the roll of the syllables, that the language has a dreamy, easy effect. Robert Moore Williams and Lester Del Rey can do that when they want. Ted Sturgeon does it at will. Other writers as good or better seem to have no sense of word-rhythm in writing at all, but have in full measure some other attribute that makes their writing pungent and pleasing. Sprague de Camp never uses the smooth, word-rhythm type of writing, but de Camp is the past master of a special art—and it, because it is unique with him, is the fingerprint of his style. De Camp makes an almost infallable choice of precisely the right wrong word when he wants it, and uses that trick with extremely good discretion, not overworking it. To point up a statement, or sharpen a phrase, to establish a character, de Camp will select a word that is entirely unexpected at that particular point; it will be some word that neatly catches the attention and strongly reinforces the phrase used.

Ted Sturgeon, as mentioned, can use that very smooth-flowing wording at will; he can also change to a sharp, arythmic style that, by its contrast, sharply focuses the particular scene he wants. In his story "It" in the old *Unknown*—and since considerably reprinted—he produces a feeling of the quiet, brooding horror of his monster by using the smooth flowing type of language. In the scene between the two brothers when one is determined to get the man, woman or thing that killed his dog, the wording is choppy, completely arythmic, and heightens the entire effect. In "Killdozer", he uses the same effects with equal success.

THE SCIENCE OF SCIENCE FICTION WRITING

Now one of the great and peculiar mysteries of this writing business that makes it a true art, and not a science, is that those tricks can *not* be used consciously, studiedly. I've seen L. Ron Hubbard applying all the skilled tricks of the trade, changing rhythm and pace, while typing on his electric typewriter at a pace of some 3000 to 4000 words an hour. When Hubbard has to rewrite a passage, he will start a couple of pages earlier, and gather momentum, so to speak, so that when he hits the revision, he's rolling at his usual high-speed pace. Not only is he not using those techniques of the good author by carefully studied application, he *can't* make them work if he slows down.

Lewis Padgett similarly writes, with full use of the mannerisms of his own unique and excellent style, at full speed. Relatively few modern authors do successfully work their material over slowly. The flow and bounce of the story depends on smooth flow and keen interest on the author's part as he writes it.

Few modern authors plot out science-fiction stories in detail before they start. Many of them, Don A. Stuart included, get a general idea, have in mind approximately the background, and the problem to be faced by the protagonist or protagonists. The final answer to the problem—the ending—is also in mind. With a vague general idea of what the story is, where it starts and where it ends, the author picks out an opening scene.

It doesn't have to be the first scene of the story. In "Who Goes There?", for instance, the proper first start of the story is the finding of the monster frozen in the ice; the story opens, though, with the later discussion of what to do with it. The opening scene should introduce the problem, and do it quickly enough, dramatically enough, that the casual glance reader will be trapped into the story before he realizes that he's not just nibbling. One all-time high in opening scenes was the starting of A. E. van Vogt's "Slan!" No one reading the first page or so but is intensely interested in why all the world is out to get that little nine-year-old kid and his mother. But the story obviously has its real beginning long before that.

Once the reader is started, good story-telling will hold him. The next important part of the story is the ending. And that is as tough, and as important as the opening. The ending must solve the problems directly raised in the story —and do it succinctly. Quick and sharp.

But it doesn't have to solve *all* problems. It can readily be set up to raise another, and obviously insoluble problem. It's fine business indeed if you can chop your story off about one paragraph before the real end of the story—but in such terms that the reader knows exactly what's going to come next, though the protagonists can't. If you can make your reader continue the story himself for one paragraph more, he'll go on thinking of your story, remembering it, even after he's finished it.

Astounding's policy is free and easy — anything in science-fiction that is a good yarn is fine by us. We do not insist on a happy ending. If the logical development of the stated theme calls for tragedy—so be it! "With Folded Hands. . ." by Jack Williamson is an excellent example of the incomplete ending and of a tragedy type story in science-fiction. The reader is going to go on thinking after he reaches the last paragraph, because the reader wants a different answer—he doesn't want a "folded hands" answer. But he is forced, by the logic of the story, to exactly the same conclusion. Folded Hands. Because of the natural mental tendency of professional technical minds, which constitutes the majority group of *Astounding Science Fiction* readers, few indeed recognized that "With Folded Hands . . ." is in fact only a personal, or small-group tragedy, and actually a racial-scale comedy, or happy-ending story. And few saw the obvious sequel ". . . And Searching Mind" coming.

A perfect example of the incomplete ending story was "Rain Check" by Lewis Padgett, the story of the immortal, indestructible being that lived in a crystal block, and was bored beyond measure—he wanted to die, but had been made indestructable. He could, and automatically, uncontrollably did, adapt to any conditions that might harm him, and did it in a matter of seconds. The story is laid about 1935; it ends with the being getting himself mailed to a museum in Hiroshima, Japan. The story isn't ended in the last paragraphs, of course, for the human characters telling the story are not possessed of the immortal being's future vision, and can't make out what it's all about. . . .

When you've got that story finished, though, there are several highly important points to remember.

Editor's live by their eyes. They protect them, and flatly, absolutely refuse to read dim typing on gray paper. Believe it or not, some incredibly horrible offenses are committed against common sense—like the bird that sent in a neatly typed job, single spaced using red ribbon on yellow paper. He got it back almost instantly. Editor's don't buy handwritten things, either; the linotypists refuse to have anything to do with it, and we don't see why an author should expect us to retype it to save him the trouble of learning his trade properly. Use a typewriter in the first place.

Don't send a manuscript rolled; only a chimpanzee is equipped to hold one in reading position, and while he has the necessary four hands, he lacks critical judgment.

But the greatest rule of all: The reason 99% of the stories written are not bought by editors is very simple. Editors *never* buy manuscripts that are left on the closet shelf at home.

If you take the trouble to write a yarn—*send it in!*

INDEX

Air Trails, 90
Alger, Horatio, 15
Amazing Stories, 37, 83, 89
American Association for the Advancement of Science, 22
American Mathematical Society, 22
American Telephone and Telegraph, 10, 89
"...And Searching Mind," 100
ARABIAN NIGHTS, 28
Argosy, 12, 46-47
Asimov, Isaac, 95, 97
Astounding Science-Fiction, 11, 51, 84, 90, 94, 97, 100
Astounding Stories, 90
ASYLUM, 54
ATOMIC STORY, THE, 90
Bell, Eric Temple (see also Taine, John, pseudonym), 21-22
Bellamy, Edward, 16
BEYOND THIS HORIZON, 12
Bigelow, Clement, 84
BISHOP'S JAEGERS, THE, 74
"Black Destroyer," 51, 52
"Blunder, The," 14
BOOK OF PTATH, THE, 52, 54-55
"Bright Illusion," 15
Burroughs, Edgar Rice, 85
"By His Bootstraps," 93
Caesar, Julius, 70
California Institute of Technology, 21, 67
Calcutta Mathematical Society, 22
Campbell, John W., Jr., 41, 43, 79, 86, 89-101
Campbell, John W., Sr., 89
"Can of Paint, A," 57-58
Chaplin, Charles, 72, 75
CHARLIE'S AUNT, 70
"Changeling, The," 58-59
CHILDREN OF THE LENS, 83
Churchill, Winston, 36
"Christmas Carol, A," 15
Circolo Mathematico di Palermo, 22
Cloete, Stuart, 13
Collier's, 12, 14
Columbia University, 21
COMEDY OF ERRORS, 71

"Conscience, Limited," 41
Constantinescue, Clinton, 84
Counts, Ed, 87
"Crucible of Power, The," 48
d'Alembert, 24
"Dance of the Hours," 72
DARKER THAN YOU THINK, 41
de Camp, Lyon Sprague, 67-76, 79, 90, 93, 97, 98
del Rey, Lester, 98
"Dick Whittington," 15
Dickens, Charles, 15
Disney, Walt, 72
DIVIDE AND RULE, 68
Dodson, Richard W., 87
Doyle, Arthur Conan, 13
Duke University, 89
DWELLERS IN THE MIRAGE, 79
Einstein, Albert, 34, 84
Elk's Magazine, 12
ENCHANTED WEEK END, 76
Enright, James, 87
"Equalizer, The," 43
Ertz, Suzan, 13
Eshbach, Lloyd Arthur, 9, 11-12, 21-22, 37-38, 51-52, 59, 67-68, 77-78, 89-90
Evans, Edward Everett, 87
"Exhalted, The," 93
FANTASIA, 72
Fantasy Press, 12, 22, 38, 52, 54, 68, 77, 90
Fantasy Review, 62-63
FORBIDDEN GARDEN, THE, 22
"Full Moon," 71
"Future History," 12
GALACTIC PATROL, 15, 83, 86, 87
Galactic Roamers, 86, 87
Gallishaw, John, 46
Garby, Lee Hawkins, 77, 83
Gernsback, Hugo, 37
"Golden Blood," 40
GRAY LENSMAN, 15
GREAT DICTATOR, THE, 72
Hart, Moss, 70
Heinlein, Robert Anson, 11-17, 79, 87, 90, 97
Henie, Sonja, 18

Hertz, Heinrich Rudolph, 28
Hitler, Adolf, 72
Holt, 68, 90
Hubbard, Lafayette Ron, 14, 15, 99
Hull, Edna Mayne, 52
Huxley, Aldous, 18
ILLIAD, 14
INCOMPLETE ENCHANTER, THE, 68
IRON STAR, THE, 22
"It," 98
Jenkins, Will F. (see also Leinster, Murray, pseudonym), 13
Joyce, James, 15
Kauffman, George S., 70
"Killdozer," 98
Kipling, Rudyard, 13, 14, 18
LAND OF UNREASON, THE, 68
LAST AND FIRST MEN, 13
Leinster, Murray (pseudonym of Will F. Jenkins), 79
LEGION OF SPACE, THE, 38, 42, 48
LEGION OF TIME, THE, 43
"Lensman" series, 83, 84
LEST DARKNESS FALL, 68
"Life-Line," 11
LITTLE CAESAR, 15
"Logic of Empire," 15
London, Jack, 15
LOOKING BACKWARD, 16
Lovecraft, Howard Phillips, 79, 81-82
MacCormac, John, 76
Mac Donald, Anson (pseudonym of Robert A. Heinlein), 11, 93, 95
MacDougall, Jeannie Craig, 78
MAGIC OF NUMBERS, THE, 21
Massachusetts Institute of Technology, 67, 89
Mathematical Association of America, 22
Maxwell, Clerk, 28
MEIN KAMPF, 15
MEN LIKE GODS, 35
MEN OF MATHEMATICS, 21
Merritt, Abraham, 79
"Metal Man, The," 38
Miller, Peter Schuyler, 74
Monroe, Lyle (pseudonym of Robert A. Heinlein), 11
MOON POOL, THE, 79
Moore, Catherine L., 15, 79
"M33 in Andromeda," 62
National Academy of Science, 22
New Mexico University, 38
New Yorker, 72
Newton, Isaac, 31
Newton's Third Law of Motion, 31
"Non-Stop to Mars," 46-48
"Note on Danger B, The," 14

Noyes, Alfred, 13
Paderewski, Ignacy Jan, 18
Padgett, Lewis (pseudonym of Henry Kuttner), 99, 100
Petrarch (Francesco Petrarca), 71
Phillips, A. M., 74
Plautus, Titus Maccius, 71
Ponchielli, Amilcare, 72
Pratt, Fletcher, 68
Punch, 75
PURPLE SAPPHIRE, THE, 21
QUEEN OF THE SCIENCES, 21
"Rain Check," 100-101
"Reign of Wizardry," 41
Riverside, John (pseudonym of Robert A. Heinlein), 11
ROCKET SHIP GALILEO, 12
Rogers, Will, 75
Roosevelt, Franklin Delano, 72
ROUND ABOUT THE CAULDRON, 68
Rossetti, Dante Gabriel, 25
"Ruling Clawss, The," 75
Rutherford, Ernest, 35
Saturday Evening Post, 12, 14
Saunders, Caleb (pseudonym of Robert A. Heinlein), 11
Scribner's, 12
Second Law of Thermodynamics, 35
SEVEN FAMOUS NOVELS, 39
Shakespeare, William, 71, 73
SHIP OF ISHTAR, THE, 79, 80
SKYLARK OF SPACE, THE, 77, 83
SLAN, 51, 52, 99
Smith, Edward Elmer, 77-87
Smith, Thorne, 70, 71, 74
SNAKE MOTHER, THE, 79
"Solution Unsatisfactory," 16, 95
Somerville, Mary, 23
"South of the Slot," 15
SPACEHOUNDS OF IPC, 77
Stanford University, 21
Stapledon, William Olaf, 13
Starzl, R. F., 79, 84
Stevens Institute of Technology, 67
"Stolen Dormouse, The," 68, 74
Street & Smith, 89, 90
Stuart, Don A. (pseudonym of John W. Campbell, Jr.), 89, 97, 99
Sturgeon, Theodore, 98
Taine, John (pseudonym of Eric Temple Bell), 14, 21-33, 79
Theory of Relativity, 34, 84
TIME STREAM, THE, 14
TRIPLANETARY, 87
"Universe," 15
University of Idaho, 77
University of Washington, 21
Unknown Worlds, 41, 90, 98

van Vogt, Alfred Elton, 51-66, 79, 90, 97, 99
Verne, Jules, 9, 28
WAR OF THE UNIVERSES, 84
Waugh, Evelyn, 73
WEAPON MAKERS, THE, 52, 62-63
Weinbaum, Stanley G., 79, 80
Weird Tales, 43
Wells, Herbert George, 9, 13, 29, 35, 36, 39
"When the Atoms Failed," 89
"Who Goes There?" 97, 99

Williams, Robert Moore, 98
Williamson, Jack, 33, 37-49, 79, 84, 93, 94-95, 100
"With Folded Hands...," 93, 94-95, 100
Wodehouse, Pelham Grenville, 71
WORLD BELOW, THE, 13
WORLD OF Ā, THE, 52
Wright, Sydney Fowler, 13
Wylie, Phillip, 13, 14

York, Simon (pseudonym of Robert A. Heinlein), 11

Columbia College Library
Columbia, Missouri